Giving Up
The Ghost

WRITTEN AND ILLUSTRATED BY

VANESSA HOGLE

First Edition:
First printing

PUBLISHED BY HAUNTED ROAD MEDIA, LLC
www.hauntedroadmedia.com

United States of America

To my son, Greyson. I was truly blessed the day you entered my life. I have watched you grow into a wonderful young man full of ideas and enthusiasm. I want many things for you in life, but most of all I want you to be courageous. I want you to know you can do anything. You have that power! You are strong in heart and mind and have so much to offer the world. Never doubt yourself. After all, you are my son, and I have tried my hardest to bestow the gift of eternal optimism on you. Use it well!

I love you,
Mom.

ACKNOWLEDGMENTS

It's been an amazing year! I want to take a moment to thank everyone for your support on my first venture, *Soulscapes*, and the continued encouragement you gave for the writing of this book, *Giving up the Ghost*. I honestly couldn't have done it by myself. Through this venture I have made a lot of new friends, and have become even closer with some of my longtime friends. I have found my reason for being, outside of motherhood, my calling in life, if you will. I am truly happy for the first time in a very long time and I owe that to all of you. I see wondrous things in the future for both my son and I, things that every one of you who have followed my progress over the last eight months have made possible. So this is a little bit of a different kind of book acknowledgement. I'm not going to single anyone out with this one, because I simply can't. I have to include *ALL* of you – everyone who has followed me on Twitter, watched my YouTube vlogs, read my blog and liked and reposted my posts on Facebook. This one is for you. You are appreciated more than you know. I hope we continue on with our little adventure, and I hope you find my stories intriguing enough to want to know more. I will continue to do this as long as I have something to say and an audience that will listen. I raise my glass to you, all of you. You are the absolute BEST!

INTRODUCTION

In my last book, *Soulscapes*, I skimmed the edges of what I do, giving a small taste of what it is like to be a remote viewer, automatic drawer and medium. I shared some of my drawings from previous investigations in which I've participated and, hopefully, gave the reader a good idea of what it is like to be involved in such things.

This book will delve a little deeper into my experiences. I am truly "Giving up the Ghost". I will lay it all out -- the good, the bad and the ugly. As much as people want to believe that the paranormal field is magical and mystical, which it can be, it is also lonely, frustrating and draining. There is nothing more frustrating than being thought crazy, or a fool or both at the same time. For those of us born into it by having special gifts, these feelings can be multiplied tenfold.

I no longer care how odd I seem, how different I can appear to others. Actually, that's not entirely true. I do care. I just choose not to hide myself anymore, regardless of the cost.

There will be a little bit of history in some parts to set up the paranormal events that involve me, so for those not expecting this, please bear with me. If at all possible I'm going to try and keep this in chronological order, but I may chatter on a bit. I want you to get to know me a little better, the way I think and why I view things the way I do. Be critical if you need to, I do not mind one bit. I want you to question me and my experiences so that maybe you will question yourself and your experiences. We'll go on this journey of self-discovery together.

I hope that by laying it all on the line about me it will make it just a little easier for others to do the same. Let's get the ball rolling to open the door for an open-minded discussion. One that is way overdue, as far as I'm concerned.

CHAPTER 1

My first memory of communicating with a ghost, vague as it is, was when I was a very young girl. You see, my grandma, Luzena Mae, and I share a birthday. I think she turned 65 the day I was born, March 14, 1972. I wasn't actually due that day, but my mother really wanted me to be born on her mother's birthday so the doctor induced her labor. Just when she thought she was going to go home empty handed I came along, a fabulous little bundle of joy with medical problems that wouldn't make themselves known until a few months later.

While I have no living memory of my "Maw Maw", I know that she used to visit me after she passed away. There is a story there, so bear with me.

My mom, my Aunt Mary, my brothers Don and Jeff, and I were all driving to the nursing home because my Maw Maw was not doing well at all. These were the days when "suicide doors" – doors that open backwards – were common on cars. As awful as the name sounds the doors actually kept my brother Jeff from getting killed. He was pulling himself up in his seat and the door flew open causing him to fly out of the car, but luckily, because of the way the door opened, he was thrown away from the wheels. My aunt slammed on the brakes as my mom flew out of the car and started running into oncoming traffic towards my brother while he rolled between the cars. Luckily she was able to get to him before tragedy struck. As she scooped him up a car stopped and she flung open the door, pushed a bunch of guns aside, and the man driving rushed my brother and her to Athens hospital while we followed behind.

Jeff was there for four long days.

Fortunately, my Maw Maw held on and the day he was released we went to the nursing home she was at. My uncle Charles took care of my brother while my mom held the hand of her mother as she passed away, February 5, 1974. Our shared birthday would have been the next month.

Family was everything to my Maw Maw. She was the mother of thirteen, with my mother being the youngest. My mother is the seventh daughter and the thirteenth child. Given the numerology, Paw Paw used to call her his little witch.

Paranormal experiences run in my family. I will incorporate some of their experiences in this book so that you have a better understanding of where, and whom, I come from.

Getting back to my Maw Maw, like I said, family was everything to her. It wouldn't have occurred to me as a child, but knowing what I know about my family and their experiences with the paranormal, I'm not surprised at all that she used to come and visit me after she died. She would have known that we would have accepted her, that we wouldn't have acted like she wasn't there like so many other people do. I'm not judging other people and their reaction to the paranormal. Not at all. But the truth is, most people have such a hard time accepting the fact that spirits, ghosts, and other entities are around us more than we would like to admit.

My Maw Maw used to come and have tea with me after she passed away. This would be my first acknowledged experience in the paranormal field. From that point on my memory is a little fuzzy. There was a lot going on in my family at the time and I think I blocked much of it out in a form of self-preservation.

My next full on memory was years later when I was about six years old, I think. My parents were divorced by then and my mother and I were looking for a house to rent closer to my Aunt Mary. I was truly excited about this because I absolutely love my Aunt Mary and my cousins, Kerry, Ricky (rest his soul) and Renee. After all, they were the ones who taught me every word to the song "Rappers Delight" by the Sugar Hill Gang. And, yes, I used to sing it all the time! Nothing would have made me happier than to be closer to them. That said, I was not excited about going to this particular house. I kept hearing the words in my head, "He killed her there." As a child, that is something that would scare you to death. Hell, it would scare an adult to death.

I argued with my mom to not make me go. My young mind couldn't understand that I had to go because there was no way I could stay at our apartment alone. So against my will I was loaded up in the car and headed off to a house that completely terrified me, although I had never even been there. As we pulled up into the drive, with the real estate agent pulling in behind us, I asked my mother again if we could turn back. I told her the apartment was fine, that we didn't need this house, we could keep looking. She wasn't having any of it.

As a parent myself now, I truly do understand where she was coming from. Even knowing what I know now I would be hard pressed to just walk away from a situation simply because someone, even my son, told me something spooky about it. That said, at the age I was then I couldn't possibly understand that.

Since I knew I was losing the battle, I asked my mother if I could stay outside and explore. Thankfully, she said, "Yes," and I set off into the backyard to look around.

From the outside it was a lovely home, nothing fancy, as we couldn't afford something like that, but it was nice and cozy looking. The humble exterior did a fairly good job of hiding the horror that lay inside.

Looking back, I am thankful that the powers that be saw fit to not give a child my age the details of an event I had no business knowing about. They told me enough to pass on the information to my mother without scarring me for life. It wasn't too long before I heard my mother and the real estate agent coming quickly out the front door, and I knew then that my warning was right. I honestly hadn't doubted it, but the confirmation made me feel slightly less crazy.

My mother and I never spoke about that incident after that.

CHAPTER 2

While I had many experiences between my youth and my teen years they are scattered and brief and don't necessarily deserve acknowledgment. Those years of my life had other influences that allowed me to unknowingly block things out. Again, looking back I am eternally grateful for this because a person can only handle so much, and I had more than likely reached my limit.

Besides all that I had going on in my life the previous years, and the reprieve I had been given from anything supernatural, the year I turned thirteen seemed to explode right in my face. I didn't make the connection at the time. I didn't understand that being female and fully entering puberty may have a lot to do with how things were starting to intensify.

My dreams started to become extremely vivid, full of color and far off places, filled with violence and love, none of which ever showed my face as I saw it in the mirror. I had about four or five different faces in my dreams. I was different ages and wearing different clothing styles. None of this I ever told a soul. You, my friends, are reading for the first time a small glimpse of how I became who I am.

This was also the time in my life that I really started having difficulty trusting people, even the simple kind of trust that you have for close friends, like trusting them enough to share some of the weird thoughts in your head and the dreams that would wake you up in a cold sweat at night. There was one particular incident that finally put me over the edge, that made me withdraw into myself even more than I already had. It was the Halloween after I turned thirteen.

For the most part it was a fairly uneventful day. There was nothing that had happened throughout it that made me think the evening would end as it was going to. Just after dinner I was taken to my friend's house along with five other girls. Our group was seven, total, all of us thirteen.

Right off the bat I'm sure you're thinking, "Whoa, what were you thinking?"

Well, if you are superstitious the numbers may have crossed your mind. I'm a superstitious person now, but I really wasn't back then. I didn't know enough about anything to be superstitious.

We started off the night by taking a walk through the neighborhood, our destination the local cemetery. It was supposed to be a spooky start to our Halloween night which, for my friends, I'm sure it was. For me, it was peaceful.

Cemeteries have always been a peaceful place for me. They're like history books telling stories you would never know if you didn't take the time to walk through them and read the headstones. I still love reading the inscriptions loved ones adorn their dead with. The words of love, and sometimes humor, that can be found here brings a smile to my face and a tear to my eye.

That day we were walking around discussing the different graves that we came across, wondering aloud at the lives they must have led and speculating about what had finally taken them. It was interesting to hear my friends as they explained what they believed to be the lives of those who had passed. They spun elaborate tales of fantastic and mundane lives alike, on murder and accidental deaths, almost always forgetting that some people actually died of natural causes.

I listened to all of this but never said a word. Something told me that it would not be a good idea to tell them that I had heard the truth as we passed most of the graves, that I could hear what had happened to people in their own words. At any given time there was a cacophony of voices and sounds telling me all the things I didn't want to know.

I tried to separate myself a little from the group so that I could get myself together. This was the first time I could remember being literally bombarded by voices, and I was having a very hard time dealing with it. As I walked further away I came across this small section of graves that appeared to be much older than the others. It was fairly nondescript. The headstones were much different than the graves that took up the remaining area of the cemetery. They appeared almost handmade. There was one that was almost hidden by the overgrowth that was only present in this area.

I got down on my knees to get a closer look, and, as the other girls approached, the images started to form in my head. I could see a little boy in what looked like an old-fashioned Christening gown. He was about two years old according to the small, hammered, metal plate serving as a headstone, and very small. In my mind I could see a thin layer of blonde hair and blue eyes. I had no idea how I knew this, but I felt in my heart it was true. I could hear my friends behind me whispering about what could have taken a child so young. I didn't have the courage to tell them what I knew, so I bit my tongue and let them finish their stories as we started back to my friend's house.

If I remember correctly the plan was to order pizza and watch scary movies while handing out candy to the neighborhood kids that came to the door. I truly wish we had kept those plans because the way things turned out left me feeling lonelier than I had ever been in my life up until that point.

I'm not really sure whose idea it was but somehow, on the way back to the house, the subject came up about trances. Maybe someone had seen one on TV; I'm not sure. Regardless, it was decided that we would give it a try and that one of the other girls and I would be the first to go. It's kind of funny now, the fact that we were so certain that we could even do it, but we were. We were a very confident group, so we decided to hold off on the pizza and get started immediately.

There wasn't a whole lot of preparation needed so we just turned the lights down a bit, and my friend and I sat on the floor across from each other. That is pretty much where my memory takes a powder and I go blank until I came to being slapped repeatedly across the face while I saw the other girls pouring ice water over my friend who appeared to be seizing. I was so dazed and sleepy that I didn't fully understand what was going on and started to get angry at how I was being treated. In my mind I had done nothing to deserve this. Then I saw the look on the other girls' faces and it stopped my complaints in their tracks.

Everyone was staring at me with the strangest look on their faces. It was as if they had no idea who I was. For that matter, I was so disoriented that I just zoned out and let them deal with our friend. When things finally seemed to calm down and they turned their attention to me I was shocked at what they had to say.

Apparently, from the moment we sat down and our eyes met the contact could not be broken. According to my friends I did not blink for almost thirty minutes and the friend who was participating with me couldn't break eye contact with me and began to convulse. The rest of the evening is a blur after that. The only thing that remains prominent in my mind is how I was treated after what had happened.

In an instant I was an outcast. Sure, I was still a member of the cheerleading squad. Most of the girls still talked to me in passing with the exception of my friend who had seized that night. It was years before she ever really spoke to me again. In fact, it was five years later when I was working at a sports bar in Wichita, Kansas, that she finally broke the silence.

I'm still not sure as to whether or not she sought me out or if it was by chance that she happened in. All I know is that I was taken by surprise when she apologized. She told me that that night she had seen something in me that scared her. What it was she wouldn't elaborate on, but that she knew I hadn't meant her any harm.

The whole apology kind of threw me because I had always wanted to know what had really happened, but, although she was sorry for how she treated me after, she wouldn't tell me why she had apologized in the first place. I tried hard to put it out of my mind but had a lot of difficulty doing so. I really felt I had done something wrong, that there was something terribly wrong with me on the inside, that I was a bad person.

It would take years before I would overcome that feeling. Almost two decades passed, if I'm honest, for me to realize that what was in me was a gift to be protected and shared with those who needed it, with those who had no place else to turn in matters that could be heartbreaking.

Not knowing that this time was coming, I turned into myself. I hid everything away that could make me appear different from anyone else. I didn't talk to anyone about it; I didn't think about it myself.

I shut down.

CHAPTER 3

I can't recall the exact moment I finally decided to let myself open up again, but I can remember the reason it happened. I had this friend whom I was somewhat close to since our husbands were in the military together. She called me one day and asked me if I wanted to go on a retreat with her. She was kind of vague about the type of retreat but I was finally able to pull it out of her. It was a pagan retreat with a group she had met online.

I must admit I was a little apprehensive at first. I had told her a little about my past and my abilities but I hadn't really gone into detail with anybody up to that point. After I had decided to go with her and the money had been paid for our cabin, I finally opened up and told her some of what had happened in my life. I was surprised at her reaction. I had expected disbelief and a little bit of scorn and mockery. What I got was understanding and something akin to awe. Once I opened up to her I felt a little of the pain from my past slip away, that feeling of being separate from everyone because of a "horrible secret".

Within days I was visiting esoteric stores in Oklahoma, meeting all kinds of people, learning that I wasn't alone in this world like I thought I'd been. It was an intoxicating experience. I was learning all about stones and their different powers, tarot cards and auras. I had my first ever aura photo taken as well. It was a wondrous time for me.

About a month after I sent in my money for the retreat we were on our way. My friend had decided that we would give a ride to another person and we stopped on the way to pick her up. It was a first time for all three of us. We spent the two hour drive to the campsite getting to know the other girl and discussing what we thought may happen while we were there. I was very excited and very scared at the same time. Even though I had become more comfortable with myself some of the old feelings would surface every now and again telling me that I wouldn't be accepted, that I was bad, and that I was too different. I tried not to let this show to the other girls and continued on with the conversation till we finally got to our destination.

When we pulled up to the campsite and I saw all the different walks of life there all my feelings just seemed to melt away. All different shapes, sizes, colors of people were there mingling together, everyone smiling and laughing while they set up tables. The men gathered wood for the welcome bonfire that we were having that night. Some of the women wore colorful scarves with little bells on them like gypsies. Some of the men wore kilts. No one seemed to look at the three of us any different than people they already knew; in fact, they seemed to welcome us with open arms.

Within minutes of being shown our cabin we were given a list of our portion of the duties for the weekend. No one there was above kitchen or clean up duty, even those whom others called the "elders". For the first time in a long time I felt at peace.

After all the introductions were made and dinner was served, eaten and cleaned up, everyone started to get ready for "circle". This was what I was really excited for because it was kind of like the opening ceremony for the weekend. It would set the mood for the events to come and bring forth positive energy for the different workshops in which we would participate.

That is a moment I will never forget – my first smudging ceremony. We all lined up to one side of the bonfire and were asked one question before we were allowed to walk through the sage smoke for our smudging. The question was a simple, but very important, one.

"How do you enter this circle?"

There is only one acceptable answer and that is, "With perfect love and perfect trust."

No other response will do, nor will any other be accepted. If you cannot enter with an open heart and mind, you need not enter.

I had no problem saying the words aloud. In fact, I needed to say them. I needed to hear others say them, as well. When the last of the people had passed through everyone took their seats so that the drum circle could start.

This was an amazing moment. They started off slowly, first one, then the others joining in one after the other. It was like a heartbeat growing stronger with every second. It was very powerful, very tribal, very primal.

Very peaceful.

We were so caught up in the moment we almost missed the oddest thing of the night. In the clearing we had made our bonfire while the moon shone down almost like a spotlight. Lightening and rain seemed to surround us completely. It was very surreal, almost as if we were being smiled upon by Mother Nature, as if she was showing her approval of our gathering with the twin tail comet that shot across the sky. She seemed to send her love to us on the wings of the lunar moths that flew around us, some as big as an adult hand. The entire scene was like something out of a movie. And I loved every second of it.

I was able to talk to others who were like me. I learned to not be embarrassed of myself or the things I was capable of doing. There were so many people there with various kinds of special abilities and special gifts that I didn't feel all that different anymore. In fact, I slept so deeply that night that when I awoke the next morning I had no idea where I was.

The next day's activities opened my mind even more as I learned about the power of crystals and Reiki. The Reiki came in handy that afternoon when I was overcome with a migraine and could not seem to get rid of it no matter what I did. The Reiki master who was there explained to me that he could help relieve some of the pain I was feeling. This was new to me, but at that point I was desperate and had no trouble crawling up on the table and letting him do his worst. I can't really explain what he did to me, as he never actually placed his hands on me. All I can say is that I felt the pain being pulled from my body like an invisible force was sucking it out. I was pretty much a limp noodle when I floated off to my cabin to rest before the evening's activities.

This was the turning point in my life. This is where the door was finally kicked open and I haven't closed it since.

I had only been lying down for a minute when I felt the motion of water underneath me. Behind my eyes I could see a shoreline far off in the distance. My view was only from my nose up, and honestly up until this moment as I write this I have never questioned why. What I could see from that minimal viewpoint was the waves crashing against the shoreline and the deepest indigo sky I had ever seen. I could feel the waves rock the boat that I figured I must be on, and far off in the distance I could see a brilliant, but tiny, flash of light.

I let the feeling of the ocean take me. I let it rock me back and forth, all the while my eyes were focusing on that tiny flash of light that seemed to grow in size with each explosion.

I didn't even try to keep track of how many times the flash occurred, I could just tell I was getting closer to it. I had no idea for what purpose this was, and I didn't care. I just knew that I wanted to see what would happen. It didn't take long, at least not to my internal dream clock, and when the flash finally became so big and so bright that I had to close my eyes against, I sat bolt upright, now awake, in my bunk.

I knew from that moment forward I would never be the same. I had no way of knowing how much things would change after that, but I knew I was a different person from the one who had lay down to take a nap. The clarity in which I could think was indescribable. I couldn't explain it, still can't explain it, but I could actually tell the difference in all of my senses.

The rest of the weekend went by in a blur of activity as I became accustomed to this new freedom. I tested out the accuracy of my sensitivities on some of the camp goers and was staggered. I still think the majority of it was beginner's luck, but I was happy about it nonetheless.

It all went by too quickly and I was honestly sad to leave, but I was happy to be getting home to my son. I hadn't been away from him before and that was the only thing that had kept that weekend from being perfect. I missed my little boy.

As we headed back home the three of us hashed out the last forty eight hours. I still kept some of the things I had experienced to myself. It was ingrained in me to do this, so I really didn't give it much thought.

After I was dropped off at my car I headed to the local McDonald's to get something quick to eat before I went to pick my son up from the sitter's house. As I was on my way there my friend whom I had went on the retreat with called me to tell me about a class on spirit animals someone was giving. I pulled into the drive thru as she was telling me this and almost slammed on my breaks. Directly in front of me, sitting next to the building, was a very large wolf. It wasn't a hybrid, nor a German Shepard; it was a wolf.

People were coming out of the restaurant and giving him a very wide berth, all the while he kept his eyes trained on me. I pulled past him and had the strongest urge to order food for him. I had already hung up with my friend so I was able to focus on the wolf and contemplate why in the world he would be there. I knew I wasn't hallucinating because it was quite obvious that other people saw him as well. I continued forward after I placed my order, kicking myself because I had become so lost in thought that I had forgotten to order him any food. I pulled forward after I paid for my meal and saw that he was still sitting there, looking at me expectantly.

Surprisingly, I didn't fear him. There didn't seem to be anything dangerous in how intently he stared at me. If anything I felt a kinship, a longing to just hop out of the truck and run along with him. I reached into my bag deciding to share some food with him after all, and I realized they had doubled my order even though I hadn't paid for it. I unwrapped the extra burger while he trotted over, then he delicately took the burger out of my hand as I handed it to him through the open window of my truck. I may have romanticized it in my mind, but I would swear he had a sparkle in his eye as he slipped away with his head held high and a cheeseburger in his mouth.

Moments later I phoned back my friend back to tell her I didn't need the spirit animal class. I already knew what mine was.

CHAPTER 4

From that point on I ran head first into the metaphysical field. If it involved anything mystical, paranormal or metaphysical, I was interested. I would go to the esoteric shops and ask questions until they would get tired of me, and I read everything I could find on the subject. I even joined a group that held discussions every week on a multitude of subjects.

I really enjoyed these meetings. They would hold classes that taught about crystals and how to charge them, and I also learned how to wrap them in wire and make pendants out of them. I started sculpting with polymer clay and made pendulums as well. I was lucky enough to even sell them in a local store.

I tried my hand at meditation.

I started to regularly have my aura photo taken and began to notice a change in the colors that surrounded me. What had started out with reds and oranges changed into blues and greens. They stayed this way for a while, then evolved into purples and white.

Before all this happened I never would have even considered having a photo like this done. Hell, I didn't even know they existed. That being said, I was able to prove to myself, and others, that I could control the energy field of the aura which means anybody can control theirs as well.

I was in the shop having another photo taken and the lady who took it noticed what she thought was an anomaly on my photo. When she questioned me about it I told her that I had put up a shield. I had been having some pretty intense and frightening dreams around that time and had tried putting up a shield to block some of it out.

Well, you would have thought I had killed someone with the lecture she gave me, something about how I was too inexperienced to know what I was doing and that I may have caused irreparable damage. I had no idea how that was possible since I was the one who did it and I quite obviously wasn't hurting anybody, not even myself. I also figured if I was the one who did it then it stood to reason that I could reverse it.

Once I felt she had vented about as much as I could take I calmly interrupted her and told her I could "fix" it. She scoffed at me. She actually scoffed! Well, if anyone knows me they know that I don't appreciate that; however, I kept my cool and told her to give me five minutes. I excused myself and went to stand in a corner and just concentrated for a minute. I'm not really sure what I did, but knowing I felt more open after I finished, I told her to snap another photo – on the house, of course, since she had made such a fuss.

It was pretty cool to see her eyes go wide as the picture developed right in front of her. On the original I still had all the colors around me, but I also had a large blank space shaped like a box that seemed to be blocking everything out. She lay the second one next to it and I was barely visible due to the white, purple, pink and blue colors that covered almost the entire picture. I have to admit I was pleased I had been able to "fix" what she thought I had broken, but the happiness seemed to stop with me. The look she gave me kind of froze me where I stood.

From that point on she was very cold and distant to me and, I admit, I was glad when I went in there a few months later and found out that she didn't work there anymore. I would never have thought someone could be so jealous of someone else in this field because we all have gifts, but I knew that was why she reacted the way she did to me. I am not so conceited as to believe that I deserved her jealousy, because I didn't. I'm no more special or talented than anyone else, yet, there it was: the green eyed monster known as jealousy. That was my first taste of it and I didn't particularly care for it.

I can honestly say that I have never had that particular emotion when it comes to another person in this field. As a matter of fact, I have always said that I would have been perfectly happy to have never seen a spirit or ghost with my own eyes, that anybody who had that gift could keep it. I would happily stay ignorant of the experience. That wouldn't end up being the case, of course, but I would've been ok with it if it had.

I continued going to group and learning from those who had far more experience than I. I had my cards read for the first time and I was told if I wanted a more accurate reading I needed to let down my guard just a bit. That was something I knew I was going to have a very hard time doing. It was ingrained in me, the need to protect myself. To be honest, to this day I still suffer from it. I'm not as closed off from everybody as I used to be, but there are very few I will truly open up to, perhaps only a handful of people, really. But I did try and open up as much as I could to the new friends I was making. I knew I needed to learn as much as I could from them.

I really enjoyed group, too, and I was able to go on another retreat with these new friends. It was some years ago and we went to Samhain. Oh, it was glorious! The energy at this particular gathering was even more powerful than the first retreat. It was the same type of situation as the first where we all had our responsibilities to make things go as smooth as possible, and it did. If I remember correctly our opening circle involved a pomegranate. It was the first time I had ever had one and I didn't think anything of taking a small bite after the person before me and then passing it on to the next person. It was as if we were one family and things like that didn't matter.

It was also rather interesting to see a bunch of big ol' burly guys, some rather good looking, walking around in kilts with t-shirts on that said, "Let freedom swing." Classic. I absolutely loved it.

Being around a group of people so in tune with nature and with themselves was very profound for me. I actually started doing my own readings on this trip and found that I was quite good at it. I was told to use the book that gave explanations on what each card meant, and I admit I did for a bit, but later on I just kind of went with whatever I heard in my head and my accuracy seemed to improve.

If I'm being honest, though, there was a bit of wine flowing that night, Boone's Farm Strawberry, to be exact. It may not pack quite a punch for most people, but for a lightweight like me, I think it loosened me up just enough to let the magic flow. Regardless of the reason for the breakthrough, I had a glorious time, one that I would have liked to have repeated, but by the time the next one came around my circumstances just wouldn't allow it.

My eyes got opened up to a whole slew of new things during that weekend, and I believe I really began to come into my own. It wasn't long after that I began to become involved with the whole "ghost hunting" thing, or at least became interested in it. Of course, I had watched all the shows, and I had my favorites along with those I thought had less to offer in the way of actual evidence. So much is hype and over exaggeration that it can raise expectations to an unattainable level. That's the one thing I promised myself I would never do. I absolutely refuse to exaggerate an experience or a message.

Dealing with a lot of the things we do is hard enough without adding deception to the list. I would rather have someone think that I wasn't any good, if I didn't get anything on a particular reading, than for someone to think I'm awesome because I lied. This field can be difficult enough. Why add to it? Those who operate like that harm an already ill-perceived field. Why add fuel to the fire?

CHAPTER 5

If I've learned anything from writing this book it's that I need to keep a better diary! I'm laughing at myself as I try and remember the chronological order of events that I want to share with everyone. So, if I don't get the order right, for those of you who know me, please be kind about it, because this is hard!

Now, if I'm remembering correctly, I believe this was about the time I decided that I absolutely had to go to New Orleans. I had dreamed about the place my entire life, so the desire to go wasn't some new obsession. The funny thing was as soon as I decided to go I was bombarded by everything New Orleans! All of the sudden it seemed like every other commercial was about the French Quarter. I was seeing Louisiana license plates all over the place, and I live in Oklahoma!

The freakiest part of all happened with my home phone. Even though I hadn't used my home phone number when I called on any of the hotels I suddenly began receiving phone calls about places to stay and attractions in the New Orleans area. That was really out of the ordinary since my home phone number was unlisted!

All these things did was confirm to me that I needed to go there as soon as possible. So, like any red blooded American girl who desperately wanted to go someplace new, I pestered one of my dearest friends, Megann Scott, to going with me. I hounded her pretty much every minute while we were at work until she finally gave in and said she would go. We set on a date six months away so that the weather would be perfect and to make sure we had enough money for the trip. I then proceeded to drive everyone crazy by counting down the number of days until the trip daily on the calendar. That part was pretty fun, I have to admit! By the time the day came around and we were supposed to leave we had added Megann's sister and sister-in-law to the traveling crew.

It was a long drive, eleven hours or so, and we rolled into the Garden district in the wee hours of the morning. Even though we had worked all day and driven all night we didn't settle down to sleep. We just changed our clothes and started walking into the quarter.

I had always had a strange fascination with New Orleans. I had always been drawn to the romanticized violent history and the stories told in the movies about it. What I hadn't known at the time is that I had some otherworldly connection to it, some past life connection that defied explanation.

I had barely made it into the French Quarter when I had people coming up to me, hugging me, asking when I was coming home. Keep in mind this was my first visit to New Orleans. I didn't know any of these people from Adam, yet I found myself hugging them back as if they were long lost friends. Somehow I didn't find such a personal gesture strange at all. Not only did the people feel familiar but the place did, too. I tried to chalk this up to having seen bits and pieces of it in movies. If that was where the strangeness stopped then I may have been able to believe that, but it's not.

We went about our business having a great time, doing everything we had talked about doing in the months leading up to the trip. We took the vampire tour and had the time of our lives. If you have never been there I strongly recommend going.

Halfway through learning all we could from a very informed tour guide we stopped at the oldest, still functioning, pub in the country, Jean Lafittes Blacksmith Shop. It's a little candlelit place that looks like it would fall over if you blew on it. We stocked up on this wonderful drink called "Voodoo" before we finished the rest of the tour.

You don't have to be a sensitive to feel the vibes coming off the streets in the Quarter. As our guide told us stories of past horrors I could see them played out in my head. I could see a young girl plummet from the window of the LaLaurie house, a house I have difficulty walking past every time I go there. You can feel the energy of all the tortured souls that the La Laurie's kept in the attic part of the house, the stench of fear and bodily fluids seeming to still permeate the air and make you gag as you pass. Many were mutilated while still alive, bones broken and left to set themselves at odd angles. It was a house of horrors, one I may be tempted to step inside someday, but only with a bad ass paranormal group with me.

I could see the flames burning through the roof of the Ursuline convent. I even have a picture, somewhere, that depicts this, and I was amazed at it when I saw it. There were no lights coming from the windows of the convent. None. So I know it wasn't a trick of the camera. The flames in the photo weren't any kind of blur caused by shutter speed. These were actual flames coming from a building that was locked up tight and completely dark.

I wanted to live in New Orleans, horrible past and all. In fact, the only thing that really kept me focused on coming home was my son, otherwise, I would have moved there in a heartbeat!

As the weekend came to a close we decided to have our last meal at a place called Mothers. I love that place! Great food, great atmosphere and they even have a guy they call Elvis working the door handing out mimosas! After we ate our last meal in New Orleans, with me holding back the tears of an emotional goodbye, we stood outside Mother's trying to figure out if we could make it to St. Louis No. 1 Cemetery, the oldest extant cemetery in New Orleans.

Now, this is where it gets weird. What I'm about to write is second hand information from the three friends that were with me, as I have *no* memory of the event. These are the events as they were explained to me:

While we stood outside the restaurant talking, I suddenly got this glazed look on my face and started to run. They said it didn't seem to matter how fast they ran after me, they couldn't keep up. They said I weaved in and out of traffic and down alleyways. I didn't seem to care about cars or trolleys as I ran in front of them. Apparently, this went on for about a mile until they caught up to me when I finally stopped outside the gate of the cemetery. My friends continued to call my name but I still didn't acknowledge them in any way. Megann said the only thing I did was hold up my hand as they walked up behind me and said, "just a minute," before walking inside and straight to Marie Laveau's tomb. Marie Laveau was a renowned voodoo practitioner in New Orleans, born in 1794 and died in 1881.

Admittedly, I did not know much about her at the time. All I know was that I "came to" standing in front of her tomb, and I had absolutely no recollection of the events that got me there. I can't describe the feeling that came over me as I stood there aside from it being a combination of peace, sadness and joy. In a way, I think we all felt it, sensitive or not. We didn't really even notice as others in the cemetery came up behind us and made their three X marks on her tomb and poured some drinking alcohol at the base of it. Once they were finished we made our marks as well, said a silent wish and left some change in honor and remembrance of her. We then we began our trek out of the cemetery.

We stopped along the way out and looked at some of the tombs. They were so beautiful! Some were quite old and somewhat rundown, but still lovely, nonetheless. Weathered by age and the southern climate, they had an ethereal quality about them. I reached down and took several stones from some of the grave sites along with some graveyard dirt for future use.

After leaving St. Louis No. 1 we returned to the hotel to get our things and head back home. We started walking down this one particular street when the oddest feeling suddenly came over me. There was a house on the right side of the street that had the windows boarded up. It was two stories high, red brick with dark green, peeling, shutters that hung askew. It was one of the most beautiful homes I had ever seen.

I was standing there with tears in my eyes when an older, very dapper, gentleman walked up to me with his newspaper tucked under one arm and a steaming cup of coffee in the other. His tweed fedora set off his beautiful silver hair and shaded his twinkling light blue eyes from the sun. Like I said, dapper. He looked at me for the longest moment, and I mean *really* looked at me. Then he said, "You know that was your house."

It wasn't a question as much as it was a statement of fact. When he said it the way he did, it was impossible to question him. He told me about how the people that used to live there had died and that their living children were now residing overseas. They still owned it but had left it to disrepair and only kept up with the taxes on it. The thought of the house sitting all broken and alone pulled at my heart even more.

I was about to question him about why he said I had lived there when he told me he'd lived on that very street his whole life, and he was over seventy years old! He told me the family had had a child who had been born to that house but hadn't lived to adulthood. He then revealed he knew as soon as he saw me that I was that child now, that the child had died when he was a teenager, but he had never forgotten her. He put his coffee in his other hand, patted my cheek and tipped his hat before he walked away.

Between me being guided to Marie's tomb and the exchange with the "dapper" gentleman, my connection to New Orleans was cemented permanently in my heart. As we drove out of town I could feel the tears well up in my eyes again, but they were mixed with tears of happiness. I knew I would come back someday.

When I got back to Oklahoma and attended the next group meeting, I relayed what had happened while I was down there to the others. It was a pretty weird feeling having people look at me the way they did. To my knowledge, this was the first time anyone had heard of an instance like this. That spooked me more than the actual event, but I kept that to myself. At that point in my life I detested letting on how much all of these experiences still frightened me, even to people who may have understood.

Besides, I'd had enough going on in my life anyway. A divorce was looming in my future and I had a small son to take care of.

CHAPTER 6

Shortly after the separation was discussed, my son and I moved into a friend's basement for a little over a month until I could move into a townhouse I found close to work. I really needed the group at this point in my life and made every attempt to be at every meeting, if possible. I even took my son with me to some of them. He enjoyed listening to everyone tell their stories and he kind of became a little mascot to the group on the nights he was there.

It wasn't long after this that there was an arrangement to investigate a house in Wayne, Oklahoma. I wanted to try out what I could do and told my friends from group to keep all information from me so I could see what I could sense on my own. I spent two weeks meditating on the name of the town and wrote out all I saw in my head. I wrote the words I heard. I drew pictures of things that made absolutely no sense to me. I didn't really know where any of it was coming from, but I knew if I was seeing it and hearing it that it had to be important. None of it really bothered me except for the intimate details that I really felt were none of my business. That was the hardest part: knowing something about someone that they hadn't told you personally. I felt like I was invading their privacy.

There was something funny that happened, however, that really helped to lighten things up for me. I was by myself one day and was taking a break from meditating when nature called. Since I was alone I decided to use the bathroom downstairs and didn't shut the door like I normally would if my son had been home. I was sitting there minding my own business when I heard something trotting down the stairs. I have a dog so I didn't give it much thought at first until I looked up to see a completely different dog sitting in my bathroom doorway panting at me and wagging his tail. I stared at him for maybe five seconds before he just completely disappeared into thin air. The odd thing was my dog didn't seem to even notice him or sense him in any way. I had always thought that animals could sense spirits even before we did, but that wasn't the case this time. Then again, she was sound asleep. If anyone knows anything about my dog it's that she is the soundest sleeper known to man!

When the day finally came to go to the house in Wayne I was unbelievably excited! I wanted to know if I had hit on any points and if my accuracy extended to this area as well as it did to reading someone's cards or auras. I drove myself to the town and parked at the restaurant where someone from the group was going to meet me and lead me to the house. This was all part of it. I had wanted all information kept from me and that included the address of the house to which we were going.

When we got there my inexperience showed all over my face as I stood and stared at the house. It was the exact same house that I had drawn in my notebook. Granted, my drawing was a little childlike, but accurate, nonetheless. What floored me even more was seeing the portrait of the homeowner's mother hanging on the wall, the exact same one I'd drawn. There was also a photo of his dog that had long passed away beforehand sitting on the end table. The photo was of the same dog I had seen in my bathroom doorway.

I was utterly fascinated by the whole thing. I had no idea what any of it meant, or if it even meant anything at all. I can say that I made a promise to myself right then and there that I would never question where any of it came from and that I would always be as honest as possible when relaying information. I really felt that it could be taken away at any time and I didn't want that to happen, not at all.

When I met the man I had seen in my visions and had described on paper it was hard not to avert my eyes. Part of me hated knowing what I knew, but I took some solace in knowing that the activity he was experiencing in the home was not of an evil nature. He was experiencing the activity because he wasn't long for this world and it was his loved ones' way of letting him know they were waiting for him.

This confused me at first, because I had sensed some evil during meditation. It wasn't long before I realized it was one of the investigators that my friend and I were working with. He was the negative presence I had been sensing for two weeks. I even called him out by his initials when my friend and I were alone, although I didn't know what his last name was. The whole evening was very exhilarating and draining.

When we finished up and felt we had passed on all the information we could, I had someone take me back to my car. I had planned to spend the drive home going over all I had experienced and try to digest it all, but that didn't turn out to be the case. I found out the hard way just how exhausting all of this can be by accidentally driving my car into a ditch. That was the night I decided I would never drive myself to another location ever again. It was simply too draining to trust myself behind the wheel afterward.

CHAPTER 7

That notion of "someday," in regards to New Orleans, came around pretty darn quick. I couldn't seem to get that fascinating city out of my mind, so I proceeded to convince my dear friend, Jana Klimeck, to take a trip down there with me.

We had met during one of our group meetings. I will never forget when she sat down next to me, before she could even say hello I said, "You're a Libra."

We both just laughed as she confirmed that it was true. From then on we were fast friends, just like Megann and I.

Jana and Megann are the two people here in Oklahoma that I never feel judged by – *ever*. They have always had my back, and I, theirs, even if we go for long periods of time without speaking. We understand how life can get in the way and things like that happen.

We planned on going to New Orleans the weekend of my thirty-sixth birthday. Just like before, there would be four of us. We were taking Jana's "mom-mobile" and going in style! I will be the first to say, no trip is as good if it isn't in a minivan! That's why I bought one. Jana and I settled in the front and spent most of the time yapping away making the drive down there go by pretty darn fast. We made good time, too, since Jana has kind of a lead foot, and we pulled into our hotel early. I had picked a new place to stay this time that was a little closer to the quarter to cut down on the walking a bit, and we parked and waited for our room to be made ready.

It was an odd little place straddling the line between the quarter and Faubourg Marigny. It kind of looms there, not really scary, but oddly, with its floor to ceiling windows looking onto the streets like hooded bedroom eyes. The interior of it can send a little shiver down your spine with the flesh tone paint that appears to be melting in odd places, like a naked body standing just a touch too close to flame. It has a fabulous little courtyard where we spent an hour or so waiting for our room, with a lovely fountain lending its own unique ambiance. When we were finally allowed into our room I felt I had entered heaven. The room was full of antiques and in the center was a king size bed that we all could fit on if we had to. Get your mind out of the gutter – there was a pull out sofa, as well. The bathroom was tiny and oddly shaped. Almost as if putting it in was an afterthought. The whole place was slightly off, yet perfect.

We got ourselves together and set out to explore. I wanted to show them all the cool places and things that I had seen on my first trip. First, we went to Jackson Square and checked out the scene where one can always expect to hear some of the best music from local musicians playing on the street. We made sure to carry some extra money to drop in their buckets. Just because someone doesn't have a record deal doesn't mean they aren't a worthy musician. It just means they haven't gotten their break yet.

There are artists lining the square and plenty of tarot readers there, as well. Choices are endless in regards to entertainment, drink and a myriad of other vices in the square from all four corners. It is a wondrous place, and I truly felt at ease there.

We made our way to a few of the esoteric shops to scope out their wares and found ourselves at a local Voodoo shop that I had visited on my first trip. I hadn't had any problems during my initial experience there, so I didn't anticipate any on this visit. I was mistaken.

I walked in and got no farther than about five feet when I felt like I had a 200 pound man sit on my shoulders. I stumbled. I actually stumbled. I told Jana I had to step outside to get some air and so I did, putting my hand on the outside wall to steady myself. That is the last thing I remember.

According to Jana and the girls it was just like my first trip to New Orleans. After a moment of my face looking slightly glazed and odd, I took off. Only this time I wasn't running. I was walking, but it was so quick that Jana called it a "super Spidey" walk that no one could possibly catch up to even if they were running. My friends were calling after me, but I didn't seem to pay any attention to them and acted as if I couldn't hear their shouts. It didn't seem to matter what they did, they couldn't catch up to me. Jana was able to keep her eye on me, at least, and they saw me go up to a house at the corner of Ursuline and Royal.

When they finally caught up to me I was frantically trying to open the front door of the place, shaking the handle as hard as I could. When that didn't work, I moved onto the windows and tried each one in turn to no avail. At some point during all of this Jana tried to stop me, afraid that someone may have thought something criminal was going on, but she said I just stared at her with absolutely no recognition on my face. I think that's the part that scares me the most, the fact that I can be completely gone in my own body, so much so that I do not recognize one of my closest friends. And this had happened to me twice within about a year.

When I finally came around I was laying on my back with my knees up on the front porch of the house with absolutely no idea where I was or how I had gotten there. That is a very freaky feeling too open your eyes and see three friends staring down at you with their mouths hanging open just waiting for you to say something. I was equally embarrassed and fascinated. I got up, brushed myself off, and said, "Lemme have it."

While they relayed to me what had happened I searched deep inside for any spark of memory I might have had about the incident, anything that would give me hope that I hadn't been completely suppressed in my own body. No such spark came. Just like the first time, I had zero memory of the event, zero emotion tied to it, zero repercussions.

I have nothing else to call these instances but possessions, yet they hold none of the negative connotations of a usual possession. I would later say in a radio interview that I thought of myself as a car. Sometimes a spirit that needed to get from point A to point B would hop in a drive for a bit. I like that way of looking at it. It allows me to sleep a little better at night.

After we had settled down from the incident, we got back on the track of celebrating my birthday in my favorite U.S. city. Of course the vampire tour was going to be on the agenda again since the gals had heard all about it and wanted to go. Truth be told, I would pay to take it every time because it's absolutely worth it. Like my trip to to New Orleans, our guide was very informed. This was not street theater. He spoke fluent Latin and knew all of the legal details concerning each horrific case on the tour, from the Carter brothers to the La Lauries. He knew it all. I believe that is something a lot of people don't realize. The stories you hear about New Orleans, fantastic as they may seem, most have some basis in fact. Every instance he told us about in his stories had legal facts to support it, including police reports, eye witnesses, and court dates. It's enough to make your head swim!

I was pleasantly surprised when we got back to Jackson Square, where the tour was to begin, and he remembered me from six months before. It was the perfect night for a vampire tour, too. There was a light rain coming down, not really enough to soak you, but just enough to add to the mystique that *is* New Orleans. We set off our way with the gals completely in awe of the tour and, if I'm honest, of the tour guide. He led us first to a small pub where Aleister Crowley had reportedly written then we were off to see and hear about more of the macabre side of the city. At the date of our tour, the last report of vampirism had been within the last twenty or so years. As much as I had a fascination with vampires, that was too recent, even for my taste. From what he told us, there had been a crew in the city filming a documentary or a movie, and a couple of girls from the crew had gone missing one night. Everyone went out looking for them and eventually found them on the steps of the Ursuline Convent completely drained of blood. Someone had cut them through each of their backs and pulled the artery from the heart through and bled them dry. I have yet to be able to find anything on the internet about this, but that does not surprise me. From what I understand about New Orleans, it is not uncommon for tragedies like this to be covered up that could hurt their tourism industry.

We spent the rest of the evening hanging with some musicians we had met and checking out some bars, all the while soaking up the atmosphere. One was called "The Dungeon," a very odd bar that doesn't open till quite late and is different from anything else I had ever seen. It housed quite a few different themed rooms where you can hang out and have a drink, but the vibe was one I couldn't get on board with. I remember needing to use the restroom and when I went to find it, the secret doorway to get to the restroom that was hidden behind bookshelves was guarded by a little man that had waist length hair and no discernible facial features that I could recognize. Needless to say, I politely made my excuses as to why I wouldn't enter and headed for the front door. There was a little tension in our group at that moment, and all I honestly wanted to do was to go back to the hotel.

When Jana and I left the building the whole "super Spidey" thing kicked in again, and I was off. I snapped back to myself as I ran right into the back of our tour guide whom we had left quite a while beforehand. He was a gentleman and walked me back to my hotel, keeping me occupied with conversation the entire way. I had no intention of asking him how far he had been from the bar, as I did not care to know how far I had traveled this time without memory. If he noticed my apprehension, he never let on.

We said our goodbyes at the hotel and I waited for the girls to get back. When they returned we all decided to go out for a walk and grab a bite to eat after we had changed.

The rest of the trip was fairly uneventful in regards to the paranormal. My only additional experience was going into a shop to get a reading and I ended up doing a reading first for the lady who planned to read me. She is the one who taught me the Voodoo spread that I use to this day.

When the time came to leave New Orleans, I was sad again. I truly loved the place and the vibe I felt while I was there, but I also knew in my heart that it was not meant to be. I would come back many times, sure, but it would always be temporary. I have made my peace with that.

CHAPTER 8

It was back to the old grindstone, for me. I got back into the swing of things with group and did my best to participate as much as I could. My son was spending a few days with his father when I left work early one day and went home to get some rest. Of course, by rest, I meant spend some time on Facebook chatting it up with friends and such. I'm not a big party gal and this was really my only source of entertainment other than my son, or hanging out with Jana and Megann, or going to group.

I had been on for a while when I suddenly felt an extremely sharp pain in my stomach that made me double over. I was practically screaming with the intensity of the pain, but it wouldn't have done any good. There wasn't anybody there to help and the place I lived in wasn't exactly the safest. I sure didn't want anyone to come running from next door! However, it wasn't just that which made me quiet my cries, it was the fact that I had no idea how I would explain that it wasn't my pain I was feeling.

I gathered myself together enough to private message the friend I had been speaking to and I began to tell her what was happening. I told her of the pain, of the name I kept hearing in my head, off the perfect description of a woman I had never seen before. I told her what this woman's father used to call her and the fact that she liked to ride horses. Every stroke of the keys was agony as I tried to breathe through the pain I was feeling. I asked my friend if she would ask any of the people she worked with if that description fit anybody they knew. I had hoped that, maybe, because I had been talking to her, that she was the link to whom I needed to relay whatever message was coming. When she couldn't tell me, "yes," I nearly cried. I knew the pain wouldn't stop fully until I had found who needed to be contacted.

You see, this is the part people don't understand. This is not something I would have ever chosen for myself. Why would anyone choose this for themselves? I may not wish this on anyone else, but I'm so used to it now, I can't imagine being any other way. People always throw around the phrase, "God doesn't give you anything you can't handle." Well, I guess I and some others are living proof of that. I was made this way for a reason and I intend to use it with as much honor and integrity as I am able to because, I feel, it could be taken away just as easy as it came.

I tried contacting a few more people to see if anyone else knew whom it was I was feeling, but, again, I came up empty handed. I finally gave up and stumbled over to the couch, hoping it would lessen a bit. I rested as much as I could but tried to keep the information sharp in my mind so I wouldn't forget anything.

Later on that night, when I felt I could finally move without throwing up, I got back on the computer and went to my MySpace page. I have weird music taste and I figured my playlist may make me feel better. When I got onto my page I saw a post from an acquaintance, a lady that I had met at a Pagan picnic a while back. Really, my only contact with her had been to get a kitten from her. I saw she had just recently, like in the previous five minutes, posted about her ex mother-in-law being taken to the hospital and was asking for healing energy for her. I volleyed back and forth about contacting a virtual stranger about what was going on, but decided appearing sane was less important than getting the message across and getting rid of the pain.

Like I did on Facebook earlier in the day, I sent her a private message. I told her everything. *Everything*. I left nothing out of the details, but I did end with, "If this has nothing to do with you and yours, please don't tell everyone I'm crazy."

I nearly fell off my chair when she messaged back and told me her ex mother-in-law had been rushed to the hospital that afternoon, approximately the same time I had felt the pain, with a ruptured stomach. She also confirmed the name, nickname, description, favorite color, hobby and the likelihood of who was speaking to me as the woman was still alive.

Now, here is what I left out of *Soulscapes*, when I described this particular instance. The lady asked me, since I was somehow connected, if I would try to send healing energy to the woman since she hadn't woken up since surgery. I had heard of this before, but had never really tried it myself. I figured you had to be pretty seasoned to be able to accomplish something like that, but I felt I had to try. I told her to give me a little bit and I would do my very best, but made no guarantees. I mean, how could I?

I left the computer again and made my way over to the couch to try and get comfortable. I was still in pain, but it had lessened some since making contact. I had zero idea what I was doing, so I just went with my gut, literally. I closed my eyes and tried to picture the inside of a stomach.

Gross, I know, but it was all I could come up with. I pictured it injured with an opening that shouldn't be there, the rupture she had spoken of. I could see the torn fibrous tissue sort of waving like a flag. I made my mind see it slowly mending back together, like a tear in reverse. I know I wasn't actually mending it, but I was sending energy to her to aid in the surgery she'd had to have because of the tear. I think the whole process took about thirty minutes, I'm not sure, but I knew I was exhausted – and the pain was gone! Completely. It was as if I had never felt it in the first place.

I received a message on MySpace later that night telling me the woman had finally regained consciousness from her surgery, and it was believed the woman would make a full recovery. Now, I am in no way saying I had anything to do with that. I am only saying I tried to do what was asked of me and the pain was now gone.

CHAPTER 9

Something about that trip to New Orleans seemed to open me up even more. I remember it was only about five months later when Halloween was rolling around and we were all gathered in the hallway at work, each of us waiting our turn for a doctor to come in and see our patients. I was standing at the entrance to our sterilization area when something came up behind me and pulled my lab coat away from my body and around to my front. I quickly looked behind me as I yelled, "Stop that!" I knew there wouldn't be anyone behind me, and I was kind of embarrassed at yelling so loud. I was even more so when I looked back and saw everyone staring at me. A few of them had their mouths hanging open, making me laugh just enough to break the tension. By this point everyone at work basically knew about me and what I did and what I had experienced in New Orleans, but most of them were pretty supportive about it. That support still didn't stop them from being completely freaked out by some unseen force trying to get my attention right in front of them.

You see, they had seen my jacket being pulled a good six inches away from my body. They had seen how some invisible hand had tugged on it hard enough to actually pull it across my stomach. I really do have to give them credit, though. The group that witnessed this was kind enough to think it was cool and not tell me I was going to "go to hell" for playing around with the unknown. Of course, I did get even more questions about it than I normally did, but I didn't really mind. It was nice to feel like I could openly talk with people about something like that. It made me feel like less of a freak.

The incident even gave some of my coworkers the courage to open up to me about their experiences and to ask for help regarding activity they had in their own homes. I made a few trips to people's houses to do readings or to help them cleanse negative energy or spirits. I enjoyed this.

Of course, I couldn't take on every request, as much as I may have wanted to. That's one of the hardest parts of being involved in this field. You really do want to help everybody, but sometimes you just can't. I had personal obligations that needed my attention. I had a family to take care of, a child who needed me to be there for him as much as others needed me to be there for them. I wouldn't have changed a second of it, either.

It was during this time that I started to notice my son following in my footsteps and began displaying certain abilities. He had made comments when he was younger about playing with his brothers and sisters when I would hear him talking in his bedroom. He didn't know then that I'd had many miscarriages before his birth, that he was, in fact, the only child I'd carried to term and the last pregnancy I would ever have. He would talk about the "white lady" that used to visit him at night, too. I knew who this was. This was my mawmaw, the one I shared a birthday with. I had no doubt in my mind. All of these incidents pieced together made a pretty impressive psychic quilt in which my son seemed to be cloaked. But even so, that wasn't what really cinched it for me.

When he was about three years old, my son started talking about someone named "Father". Now, keep in mind that I would never allow anything around my son that I would consider, in any way, dangerous. He never gave any indication that he was afraid, and I didn't sense anything negative in the house. He said Father came to his dreams. He described this figure to me and said he would talk to him and watch over him.

Admittedly, I was a little perplexed. I didn't understand why I couldn't see Father. I didn't understand why he wasn't coming to me as well. Just in case there was something negative that I couldn't sense, I did teach my son a very simple way to protect himself if he ever felt threatened.

This went on for a couple of years with my son talking about Father off and on. It didn't really reach its head until one night when I was downstairs in our townhome watching T.V. and talking on the phone. My son came down the stairs from his room and looked at what I was watching and said, "See, momma! There's Father! Well, not him, but that's how he died, momma!"

The movie I was watching was *Dracula 2000*, and the scene was the one in which Judas is hanging from the tree at sunset. My son had never seen that movie before, but he was so adamant, and a little bothered, by actually seeing on T.V. what he had already been shown in his dreams. I knew he wasn't making it up because I had been told the story by him for a couple years by that point. He had told me from the beginning that Father had been hanged and that he'd been there when it happened. He said he was fourteen at the time and hadn't been able to stop it, that no one had listened to him. He said that when Father came to him at night it was to protect him, to watch over him and give him advice.

In all honesty, I almost felt I needed to tell Father, "Thank you." My son is one of the most loving, compassionate, empathetic and caring individuals I know. If Father had anything to do with that, then he deserves some thanks.

Even though my son was starting to show some of the same abilities I possessed, that didn't mean that I was willing to take him with me when I went on investigations, but I did continue to take him to meetings with me on occasion. He really seemed to enjoy it and was another thing we could share with each other, another bonding moment.

That said, I was glad I went to one particular meeting by myself. It was at this meeting that we talked about going on another paranormal investigation, but no significant details were discussed since it hadn't really been decided whether or not we would actually go. It wasn't until a few days later that the decision was finally made that we would go to a place called Eldorado a couple of weeks later. This was another time I planned on checking my accuracy, so I asked the group to keep all information away from me until we went. I spent two weeks doing as I had done before. Writing down everything I heard and drawing out pictures of what I saw during meditation and dreams.

Now, this is where it gets weird again. I wish I could say that when you get a message or a vision that it will always make sense. Unfortunately, that isn't the case, at least it isn't for me. No, I just have to be different. I think the "powers that be" are testing me constantly to see if I can figure out what in the hell they mean when they send me a vision.

While I was trying to sense as much as I could so that I could contribute on this investigation, I had a dream. It was the strangest thing. I could see myself walking through this very large warehouse type store where boxes were stacked floor to ceiling with some missing here and there. In those empty spaces were cats. They sat there watching me as I walked through the building. I could see a woman ahead of me. She had her hair pulled back with the most beautiful cross barrettes. There were three of them. They looked like they were hand carved out of wood, kind of 3D style. I remember being completely mesmerized by them. She never looked back at me, so I have no idea what she looked like. I only knew that I had to follow her, and I did exactly that. We passed through a set of double doors at the back of the building, but she disappeared right in front of me and I was, all of the sudden, in a Target Store dressing room. It was disorienting at first, but then I began to laugh because everyone who was sitting there waiting to change was holding a little dog. Most of them were Chihuahuas, and from what I could gather, the dressing room was for them because they were all wearing clothing. Then a little Chihuahua came trotting out of the dressing room wearing some type of dress with little bows on it. So, yep, that pretty much cinched it.

In an instant it was all gone – the store, the warehouse, the dogs and cats. I was standing in darkness, alone, then I came to in my living room. I wasn't disoriented since I knew I had been dreaming. I'd had complete control of my faculties in the dream as well. I never once felt like I wasn't in control. I gathered my thoughts and kept the images fresh in my head as I began to draw out the things I had seen. As I did this I began to see two different houses in my mind. One appeared to be quite old while the other had a more modern look to it, something maybe from the 1970s. I drew both of them out along with the crosses, the cats, a noose and some other things. I wrote down everything I had felt and heard, as well, and put it all away until the day we left to go on the investigation.

One of the group members came to pick me up and we set off to get the others. Four of us were going to drive together while the rest followed in another car. We were having a good time on the drive, even made a quick stop for snacks before we headed back on the road again. I remember we were about halfway there when I started to feel quite strange. My heart started to race and I couldn't catch my breath. I started shaking and felt like I was going to pass out. I realized I was in the midst of a panic attack, which was completely unlike me. I was not then, nor am I now, prone to panic attacks. I'm pretty good at keeping a level head about things and I don't get too terribly over excited. Yet, that definitely was not the case that day. Everyone in the car did their best to calm me down, and it worked a little, but I couldn't shake the feeling that I had, a terrible feeling of foreboding. That feeling stayed with me, but it did subside some until we got to the town of Eldorado.

As we drove into town there were two grain towers standing sentinel on the left side of the road. The darkness seemed to start there, a heavy oppressive feeling that seemed to envelope the car. We all felt it. The tension in the vehicle increased as we neared the house we were going to investigate. The bottom of my stomach dropped out when we pulled down the street and I saw cats lining the opposite side of the road and the two houses I had drawn were sitting kitty-corner facing the destination house. I will admit it, right here and now, I did *not* want to get out of the car, much less go into that house. It wasn't that it looked particularly scary, because it didn't. The problem was what I felt when I stared at the house. I felt sick and dirty inside, like I would be "unclean" if I went inside, unsafe.

One of the team members from the group that invited us came over to me and asked me what I thought of the place. I handed her my notebook. I honestly didn't want to touch it again, nor did I want to tell her what I was really feeling, but I knew I had to. That was what I had gone there for, anyway. I told her that I wasn't comfortable saying, but she said I had to, so I told her exactly what I felt when I looked at the place.

I saw fire and brimstone in the front, orgy in the back. The place had dirty preacher written all over it. It was then that I found out there used to be a church on the property. That only made me want to put off going into the house even more, so I walked around to the backyard and about had a heart attack. Do you remember when I described the dream I had with the woman I was following with the three carved cross barrettes? Well, when I walked into the backyard I looked up at the roof of the house and my breath caught. There, just like I saw in my dream, were three crosses. The shingles had separated on the roof in three places making it look like there were three 3D crosses, one on top of the other. It was yet another thing that made me want to turn tail and run, but I didn't.

We continued the investigation and I, with some help from the other investigators, was able to confirm a lot of what I had written in my notebook. There were quite a few sensitives on this trip and we all had something to offer. I remember one of the investigators had a vision about peacocks and had even pulled a tarot card depicting them before we left. Sure enough, there was a framed picture of peacocks at the top of the stairs in the house. It was upstairs where we set up shop for part of the investigation.

There were three of us in a room where it was reported that a fair amount of paranormal activity had happened. There was a very cold feeling to the room, one that seemed to settle deep in your bones and stay there. You could feel the vibrations in the room, a feeling I wasn't exactly comfortable with. One of the investigators brought this device that had these little light bulbs that lit up when a spirit communicated with you. I can't recall using one of these in the few previous investigations I had done, but I was super impressed with it. As we stood in the bedroom and began to ask questions out loud, we noticed that slowly but surely the lights would respond to us. If we were quiet, they didn't glow. If we asked a question, they reacted. We were even able to get it to light up the number of lights we requested. This was amazing to me. These were intelligent responses; something that even I, a novice, knew was very rare.

When we had gotten as much as we could from the upstairs, we headed downstairs to see what the others had discovered. They had hit the mother lode on evidence as well and had gathered on the front lawn to wait for us to come down and talk everything over. We decided to do one last EVP session in the front yard. While we did this we were looking at footage on a laptop that the other team had gotten on a previous investigation of the place, still shots they had taken. There was one pic that had this weird light on it and I said, out loud, the first thing I heard in my head.

"They hung him there," I said.

A few minutes later, when we were reviewing the recording and we heard something that sent shivers down my spine. When we got to the part where I said they had hung him there, about two seconds later we faintly heard, "They hung me."

I started to shake. An absolute horrible feeling overcame me and I felt the urge to scream rise within me. At that instant I felt a searing pain slice through my left thigh as if I had been filleted open by a blazing hot knife. I did start to scream then. I screamed with about a dozen people staring at me in shock. I wanted to run and started to do exactly that when something caught my eye. About 100 feet away I saw one of the most beautiful creatures I had ever seen. It was a snow white wolf, large and almost glowing in the darkness. It sat there, staring at me, and I felt as if it were summoning me to its side. I started toward it and I heard the others yell at me to stay where I was. At that moment I realized they saw him, too, and I didn't feel quite so crazy.

I walked closer to him anyway, paying no mind to the warnings from the group. When I got within about fifty feet of him I stopped and stared into his eyes. I can't really say I felt or heard a verbal exchange, but I knew what he wanted. After a minute or so, I turned around and walked slowly back toward the cars parked in the driveway. I could feel everyone's eyes on me as I got into the back seat of my friend's car. Rolling down the window, I stuck my head out and gave the wolf one last glance. Shocking the hell out of me, he nodded his head and turned and walked away as if he were pleased that I had listened to some unspoken command.

It wasn't long after that when we made another trip to the same location to film a show for Animal Planet called the *The Haunted*. That particular trip was more about filming the show than it was about investigating, but it was fun. I had the pleasure of meeting new people from across the country and getting an idea of how it works behind the scenes of a television camera. Animal Planet put us up in lovely private rooms, as well. I was surprised to see something so nice in a place so rural, but I may be able to chalk that up to my lack of luxury experience more than anything. At that point in my life I wasn't exactly a seasoned traveler, a fact I had high hopes to change in the future.

After we finished filming for the day we all gathered in one hotel room to talk things over, and I did some automatic drawing for one of the other sensitive investigators there and the demonologist that had come in from up north. I felt like a child pleasing an adult when they told me that I was accurate. I so wanted to impress other people and prove my worth to the group, and I was in awe of these two because they had so much more experience in the field than I. They had seen and heard and felt so much in their years, and it fascinated me to hear about it.

It was a fun couple of days and, when it was over, I was kind of sad to see it end. I didn't really know what to expect, when it came to the show. I knew I wasn't an actual member of the group that went down there, that I was more of a guest psychic, so I can honestly say I had no expectations on the outcome. That said, when everybody had gathered for the premier of the show at a local pizza joint, I sat with my guest through the entire show waiting for a clip of me and was stunned. I was the only one missing from any airtime.

Nothing.

I did hear parts of my reading being used, but I was not mentioned at all, not even as an afterthought. This was my first time getting a real taste of the dark side of the paranormal field. It wouldn't be my last, or the most bitter. I tried to tell myself that it was because I wasn't an actual member of the team and that was why I was cut out, but if that was the case, why have me go all the way out there in the first place? I didn't just tag along. I was specifically asked to come, by name, from the leader of the paranormal group heading it. I did later find out that I was purposefully cut from the footage by the same person who asked me to be there. The reasons I've been told were selfish in nature, and that's fine. Mine has never been an ambition to seek the spotlight. In fact, until now, it has been the exact opposite. I've done everything I could to stay out of the public eye as much as possible. If I'm honest, I'm not sure if I've been that way because of that show or in spite of it. Maybe laying low was my way of keeping safe and not getting my feelings hurt again. Who knows?

It took a little bit to get over that slight, I'm ashamed to admit, but I am only human. I can't say I ever coveted notoriety for anything I ever did. No, I would say it was the exact opposite. But that doesn't mean that I freely give away such a personal part of myself for someone else's gain.

CHAPTER 10

Even though I was still a little miffed, I continued to do some investigations here and there, although not with the same paranormal group. I suppose I should have made a distinction earlier that there was a difference between the Pagan group meetings I was attending and the ghost hunting group I sometimes went with, although some of the members overlapped. The ghost hunting team I was spending time with at that point had branched off from the previous group that ran the investigation in Eldorado.

This happens a lot in groups in which dissension and resentment tends to fester and grow. It really used to bother me. In a way, I guess it still does, but I have learned it's normal. It really is. This isn't rocket science or brain surgery that you can go to school for and study. Some people will spend their entire lives waiting desperately to have an actual paranormal experience, while others will have them daily. Sure, there are ways you can open yourself up to be more receptive, but that isn't a guarantee. There are all kinds of "gifts" out there that people have. Some may only have one, some may have multiple. It's a recipe for resentment and jealousy if you let it get the better of you, so don't.

One of the investigations I went on was a public investigation we held to raise money for a location in

Hennessey, Oklahoma. This was really quite fascinating. It was the second public event I had been a part of and I was really excited about it. In these instances I don't do anything special like meditate. I wanted to go in and just see what I got, and the place was quite fantastic! It was an old saloon that was currently being used as a local watering hole and rec center. We split up into three groups with each group taking a different section. One took the cellar area, while the other two split the main floor and the upstairs.

The group I was with took the upstairs first. I can't really say it was a creepy place, but there was a definite heaviness to it. In some areas it was very difficult to breathe. All of the guest took pictures and asked questions, and most importantly, stayed quiet during EVP sessions. I was really impressed with how my group was at giving a guided hunt, and also how informed and respectful the guest were in regards to the history of the place.

A few people from my group and I broke away from the others to wander around the upstairs when we walked into a room that faced the street. From the second I walked through the door I could feel the heat on my back. Like an open flame up against me, I felt the fire burning my skin. There wasn't exactly pain with this, which is odd. It was just the feeling of it being there, but I was numb at the same time.

I asked the others that were with me to feel my back and tell me if they felt anything. Each one of them said it felt like my back was on fire. I purposefully hadn't told them what I was feeling. I wanted to know if it was me having an overactive imagination. However, I had no way of asking them if they could tell I felt like I had a noose around my neck. That feeling I kept to myself. I left the image of a woman being strangled and abused in the room as we left to rejoin the others.

While we made our way to the stairs, a daughter of one of the team members and I saw something that I still have yet to explain. Hovering about a foot off the floor was a crazy iridescent light. It was about eight inches long and seemed to slither like a snake.

Now, before you say it had to be someone with one of those hidden laser pointers, I've already thought of that and can say, without a doubt, that is impossible. You see, we chased it. We were ahead of everybody else and the light was ahead of us, hovering and slithering. It moved ahead of us faster and whipped around the open corner of a doorway into the room that faced the street. There is absolutely no way anyone could have gotten a laser beam to curve around a corner with us blocking their view of the door. We could hear noises in the room as we entered, but found nothing. It was just a room full of boxes and junk, old furniture and files. The light had just disappeared into thin air! On that note we started down the stairs as the other group made their way up.

We finished up the rest of the tour and then everyone gathered on the main floor to discuss all that had happened. After we gave a small presentation to the group of guests we spent about an hour or so going through their cameras and phones and discussing their photographs. A number of people had actually captured images that could be construed as evidence, and that was good! The last thing you want is for people to be disappointed when they come to a guided event like this even though you can't really make paranormal activity happen on demand. All in all, I would say the evening was a smashing success.

As time passed the team was able to go on more and more investigations. I did as many as I could, but for the most part, I remote viewed for that team. Between work and being a single mom, I just couldn't take the time away, but I could view photos on my phone that they would send me and I would give my reading from those. I did enjoy doing this, but I missed going to locations, too.

When the time came for an investigation at the University of Oklahoma, I jumped at it. I didn't live far from there at all, and knew that the travel time wouldn't keep me from home for very long.

I may have lived close to campus, but I didn't really know anything about OU at all. I'm not originally from Oklahoma, nor am I a huge Sooners fan, so I don't really pay attention. I mean, I like them well enough, but I don't follow any news on the team or the campus.

As per previous investigations, information on the location was kept from me and I was picked up from home instead of driving myself. We pulled up to the building and got out to wait for the others who were on their way. From the outside, the building we were to investigate was rather unassuming, not foreboding in any way. However, when the rest of the team arrived and we were let inside, the reasons behind my sleepless nights the previous two weeks became abundantly clear. I was kind of irritated when I looked over at one of the other investigators and asked, quite pointedly, "Why the hell did you bring me to a hospital?"

I wasn't at all pleased, but I also knew it wasn't their fault. They couldn't help my reaction to hospitals. I had spent the last two weeks tossing and turning, hearing, "Pick me, pick me!" in my head over and over like I was standing in the middle of an auditorium full of people.

The guys were talking about the different noises and strange happenings people had talked about when referring to the building. The sound of a skateboard or skates going down the hallway when no one was there was frequently reported by staff. In actuality, it was gurney wheels they were hearing. When I said that may be it, everyone agreed that made sense.

It was an interesting place, if not overly active. We gathered in the lower conference rooms to discuss how the evening would go. The two older ladies that were in charge of the place sat in on the meeting, as did the journalist who was writing an article on us. I took a seat next to the ladies and kept my mouth closed. I didn't really like to get too involved in the running of things. Leave that up to the head honchos, I always say.

So, I sat there listening to the group answer questions the journalist had, and I answered when I had to. This was extra hard since I was doing my level best to keep my thoughts from showing on my face. As I sat there I had a symphony of water sounds running through my head. I could see it running down the walls, could almost feel it under my feet. I was getting increasingly uncomfortable and decided to finally say something about it, so I looked to the ladies next to me to ask them. I found they were staring at me in the oddest way. The one closest to me asked if I was ok.

I guess I hadn't done as good of a job keeping things hidden as I'd originally thought. I told them I was fine, but that I did have a question I would like to ask them. I started with my usual, "Please don't think I'm crazy..." then asked if they could hear any running water in the room. They exchanged a look and then said me, "Why do you ask?"

I told them all I was hearing and seeing and watched their faces change from worry to disbelief. One of the ladies seemed to get visibly nervous and I felt instantly guilty for saying anything. The one who seemed to be a little more comfortable with the situation said that she was amazed, that she hadn't really believed in any of it till that moment. I asked her what she meant by that. That was when she told me that a few months prior to our investigation; pipes had burst in the building and had flooded the entire room in which we were now sitting. They said there was no way I could know that because the information had not been public knowledge.

They perked up a bit after that and seemed to be more interested in what was going on. It's always cool when you can open someone's eyes for the first time in the paranormal field. It's like watching an awakening when a person realizes that there are things they cannot explain and, instead of trying to discount it, they accept it.

We continued our investigation, with the guys gathering whatever evidence they could before we headed to the local pancake house for a late night snack and discussion. It really was a fun night. After that we headed back to our own homes and waited for the article to come out. When it did, I think the group was quite pleased, as was I. The journalist did a really good job of being opinion free and not critical of the process. He had kept a pretty open mind through the whole thing. He also got a pretty good photo of us to accompany it!

I didn't do a whole lot with the group after that as people started to go their own separate ways. Some moved out of state and some moved on to create their own groups. I did, however, continue to read for others and to remote view. A few of those readings I wrote about and illustrated in

Soulscapes, as I did with some of my dreams and meditations.

One of those dreams had involved death masks flying through the sky from a long distance. I had no idea at the time what it meant. I just knew it was important. Unbeknownst to me, that dream would turn out to be prophetic, although I wouldn't discover this for a few years.

CHAPTER 11

For a while I started to shut down again. Not being with a group and not wanting to be with a group because of how things often turn out kind of makes you do that. Plus, what I think might have been considered "cute" about myself to some, had long since become something that was considered interference, a burden of sorts, no longer the novelty and interesting topic of conversation it had been in the beginning. So I started keeping things to myself again, my dreams, my nightmares, things I would see and hear. There was a whole slew of people I was not really allowed to discuss things like this with, and that hurt. It's not like I was an axe murderer, or a criminal. I was just different. And I began to feel more different and isolated by the day. I did this for years. I would have a small burst of defiance where I would say to hell with it, and do my thing, but for the most part I conformed.

You're gonna laugh when I tell you what snapped me out of it. Are you ready? It was the show *Ghost Whisperer*. True story! I had never watched it when it was a weekly show, but when I got Netflix and saw that they had it, I started watching. I was hooked instantly.

Like a silly gal I actually told myself that if Melinda could do it and not be considered completely crazy by a whole town, then so could I. Silly, right? Maybe, but it was exactly how I felt. Now, I didn't dive in head first, but I did keep my feet in the water – at least in the shallow end.

I started doing readings online more often. I joined a psychic community on Facebook that had members from all over the world that numbered in the tens of thousands. A couple of those readings are in *Soulscapes*, as well. I had the opportunity to meet some really interesting people who have amazing gifts! I was fortunate enough to be accepted by them and learn from them. Of course, there were people on there who had that "Holier than thou" mentality, but I just didn't interact with them. Meanwhile, I had continued discussions with my friend who is an author and was starting up his own publishing house. He was still interested in me writing a book and illustrating it, so I decided to finally jump fully in the water and say, "What the hell – let's do it!"

I started to go back over eight to ten years of investigations, dreams and meditations, in my head. What a chore that was! The word "draining" doesn't even begin to describe it. I was a little surprised at how much of it I had retained in my memory since I had not really kept any good notes on the subject. In fact, most of my original drawings ended up with whatever group I was working with, or whatever person we were helping. Some of them were pretty fun to do because not all had, what one would consider, "bad" spirits attached to them. Some were downright hard. Granted, as I relived the moments, I didn't have to feel the pain that was inflicted on others like I'd had to before, but I did feel a milder version of it. It ended up being kind of therapeutic, actually. I felt myself letting go of a lot of resentment on how things had gone during the time of some of those investigations. It was good for me, I think.

By this time I was starting to get a little antsy about the direction my life was taking. I could see this bright future out there but had no earthly idea on how to attain it. I did know my first book was a step in the right direction, not necessarily the selling of it, although that is nice, but the completion of it. I desperately needed to prove to myself that I could do it, that I had it in me to not give up, that wanting more out of life didn't make you a bad person, it made you a better person.

When I was finishing up the last bit of that I did another thing I said I would never do. I started a Twitter account. To be fair, you must know that I had despised Twitter for years. I even hated the word "tweet". I'm not really sure why, either. I don't claim to have an explanation for it, but there you have it. So, when I finally did it, I was as surprised as anyone. It took me a while to figure it all out, too. I'm not ashamed to admit I'm not the most tech savvy person out there.

I started looking through all of the different people on there and came across some paranormal groups that looked pretty interesting. I went through pictures they had posted and contemplated commenting on them. I went back and forth with this for a bit. I wasn't really sure if I wanted to even post to a group because I hadn't had the best experience in the past when it came to group dynamics. Fascination over the pictures they had posted finally won out and I sent a mini reading on one or two of them. I just listed what I felt when I looked at them and what I saw actually in the pictures. When I was done, I put my phone down and continued with doing whatever I had been doing, which was to try and finish my book. I honestly didn't expect a response from what I had posted, so you can imagine my surprise when I got just that.

I just kind of stared at my phone for a minute in a, "What do I do now?" kinda way. This is the part where I could just end this book right now by saying, "And the rest is history!" but I won't.

What I can say, and what I didn't know then, is that this was a defining moment in my life. You hear people say all the time that it's the little things that make a difference. Hell, posters are printed with inspirational quotes about taking chances and new memes are created everyday about it and being shared all over social media. Well, this isn't a meme, and it isn't a poster, but it's true, nonetheless.

Had I not have taken a chance on looking like a kook, I wouldn't have met some of the nicest people I've ever known. I wouldn't have made such good friends that, even though they live all the way across the big pond, I talk to them almost every day. I've met their families. I've done readings for them and their families. In turn, they have made me feel welcome in a field where rivalry runs rampant, made me part of a team that I am proud to say I belong to. In the months since we have met, I have had the honor of assisting on investigations that air weekly on Livestream and then are posted to YouTube for later viewing and scrutiny. It really has been an amazing adventure!

CHAPTER 12

What surprised me even more was waking up one day and seeing them tweet about the upcoming release of my book. I never expected that. It honestly brought tears to my eyes. I wasn't being used, not that I thought they were doing that, but that was kind of what I was used to. Doing what I do it is a rarity to have someone do something nice for you without some ulterior motive. They even bought one of the first copies of my book. I suppose this is where I should introduce them so ya'll can put some names to these fabulous people. The members of NP Paranormal are Richard Burrows, Karl Porter and Dave Newton. Three pretty swell gents, in my book.

It was the fellas that I met first off as I started to follow their investigations, pitching in where I could. If memory serves, one of the first investigations I did on Livestream with them was Wards End Cemetery. Like before when I had worked with other groups, I had them keep their prospective location from me. I only got to see where they ended up at the same time everyone else did.

For those who haven't seen it before, Livestream is interactive. The viewers can type in comments to the fellas and they will respond live so that the viewers can hear. This cemetery was pretty cool, too. They got a ton of EVPs (electronic voice phenomena) including one saying, "It hurt", when they asked about the lobotomy I felt had happened. That was the only thing I knew to call what felt like a spike going into the back of my skull.

It was all unbelievably fascinating. This was the first time I had ever gotten to view an investigation in this manner. It also made my participation much more fulfilling since I was able to interact in real time, seeing the guys investigate and not just reading still shots from camera phones. That experience gave us a lot to talk about and made me even more excited to watch them again.

I hope I get the order of locations right but, if I don't, please blame me, not the guys. If I'm remembering correctly, I think Terminal Gravity was next. This was one they did at the Cannon Brewery, one of my favorites, for sure, simply because it was pretty active on my end.

I had woken the morning of the investigation hearing explosions in my head, but not having any idea what in the hell it could mean. During my day at work I'd had the name "Bill" running through my head without reason. I also felt like there was some connection between the guys and the place they were going to be investigating that evening. I sent them everything I had gotten that day in a private message from the explosions, to "Boss man Bill", to architecture descriptions and the possible personal connection. I couldn't wait till I got home so I could lock myself away with my phone and some headphones. I had already told everyone that I was going to start taking a couple of hours for myself once a week and this was how I planned to spend it.

I'm not going to lie, I was unbelievably tickled when Karl confirmed that Richard, AKA "Buzz", used to park his lorry at the brewery confirming the connection, but he also confirmed the stone structures I had seen. The brewery was named Cannon Brewery, so that explained the explosions I had heard in my head. It was a little later in the investigation when the "Boss man Bill" part was confirmed. They found a document dating back to when the brewery was open that had Bill's signature on it. All in all, a proper good night.

Dave did most of the filming that night and didn't have much camera time, but that would change in the future when the fellas started to bring along Abby Thompson to handle the camera like a pro. Abby rocks, for those who don't know, and the guys are lucky to have her along when she comes. When she's not with them and just on Livestream like the rest of us, she still has their back and keeps an eye on their gear for them. I could never keep up with it like she does. A true ace, she is.

The next investigation really cemented my need to see this particular team succeed. Not only are their ethics above reproach and they can get evidence live that a lot of groups would have to fake in editing, but they got guts and are dedicated to their fans, too. There was one weekend when Dave and Karl were unable to investigate due to previous commitments, so Richard went at it alone for the sake of the fans at the one of the most haunted locations in England, the Derby Gaol.

I have to tell you, this one was a tough one for me. I kept seeing a man in my head, and I couldn't decide if he was good or bad. I drew him out and took a picture with my phone. I sent it to the guys on Twitter hoping that maybe it would help in the investigation. There were other drawings, as well. Disturbing ones that gave me nightmares not to be believed. I dreamed of them hanging a woman and then quartering her. I could actually see her limbs lying on the ground beneath her. It was almost too much to bear, and the investigation hadn't yet started.

By the time it finally did, I felt like I'd been run over by a Mack truck. Almost from the moment Richard got there things started to happen. I've been doing this a long time, long enough to know what is dust and what isn't. Light anomalies and weird shadowy, slithery, things seemed to shoot and slide from one corner of the condemned cell to the other. The coolest thing was happening, too. I had already wondered about some past life connection with the guys because of how well we all seemed to get along. This particular location seemed to confirm it. I would feel something happening, type it in, and then watch Richard feel the same thing on screen before he ever read what I wrote. It was really amazing – frightening, but amazing.

The evidence that night was pretty spectacular, too. He caught an amazing EVP saying, "*Murder,*" in response to a question he had asked. It was an intelligent, loud and angry, response, definitely a success!

The next time The Gaol was visited it was by Karl and Richard. This was when I found out that my mask dream was prophetic. What I had not known the time before, when Richard had been there alone, was that they had something pretty unreal in a glass case for visitors to see. As they started to Livestream the next time they were there, they took the camera over to the box and gave the world an excellent view of these creepy, white death masks. They were eerily similar to the ones I had dreamed of years before and had drawn out. Those drawings were now out there for everyone to see in my first book! If I had any doubts as to what I should be doing, and with what group I should be doing it with, they were forgotten right then and there. In that moment I knew I was exactly where I needed to be.

The guys went on to have one helluva night, getting plenty of EVPs and video to post on YouTube. Each episode they did had a growing list of followers. When Dave wasn't able to be on location, he was directing traffic and offering support as the NP representative on Livestream.

He was also intricate in getting me back into doing readings – a lot of readings – starting with his niece, Corina. What a doll! I'm actually smiling as I write this because neither one of us realized the Pandora's Box that was being opened when word got out that I did tarot readings. Looking back, it really was quite comical. What started out as one or two turned into over forty readings in three weeks! Every time I turned around my Twitter direct message notification was going off. I woke up to it, and went to sleep (barely) to it. I have the hardest time saying no, and if you could have seen me during that time period, you would understand how much energy was lost by doing that many readings. I began to resemble the walking dead.

I loved every minute of it.

Sure, I was beat down and pretty tired, but I was doing what I was good at. I was able to give some people peace, others hope and a few answers to questions they couldn't really ask anyone else. It made me feel really good inside. I felt needed. Don't get me wrong, as a mother I know I'm always needed. My son is my world and the reason I work my ass off every day so that I can provide for him and do things with him that would be impossible otherwise. But I know, one day, he's going to get to that age where mom is no longer cool, that fun outings with me will take a backseat to friends and girlfriends, and that's okay. It's the way it's supposed to be. Knowing that doesn't make it any easier to deal with, and I don't want to be one of those women who wake up one day and wonder where everything went, where my hopes and dreams went that were only for me. A few hours out of the week to keep those dreams alive is a small price to pay.

So, I continued to read for the team whenever I could and kept in touch on, almost, a daily basis. Things really started to take off for me with their help, and I started a blog under the name hottamalered. I was able to vent out portions of my experiences on there to see how people would respond. I was very pleased with how it all went, too. I started to get a pretty steady stream of followers on the blog and on Twitter. I have to admit, as much as I had been against Twitter in the previous years, it has been my champion when it came to getting my name out there. I've met and talked to people that I never would have before. For that, I am grateful.

It also allowed the viewers of the Livestream show to talk about their experience after the fact. And, trust me, did we all have things to talk about! I will completely admit to being a little bit biased when I say what my absolute favorite investigation was.

The guys, Karl and Richard, started the show one night at an absolutely beautiful location, although it was so dark. I will never forget the night because Jana and I were going to have dinner at our favorite Mexican restaurant before we went back to my place to watch. Murphy's Law being what it is our waiter was slow as molasses so, of course, we were running super late. We both had to pull out our phones at the dinner table to try and start watching there. The signal was for crap inside the restaurant because it was inside a mall, but we did the best we could. From the moment they announced they were at the "Nine Ladies Stone Circle" the game was kind of on for me.

Jana and I hauled ass out of the restaurant as soon as we got our check and sped back to my house. I could hear chanting in my head and was desperately trying to utilize the voice to text option on my phone so that I could send it to Livestream.

"Bring the light, the dark, the blood, the sex and see the fire. For three will come and turn the soil. Bury thy funeral pyre."

It finally went through as we pulled in to my drive and we rushed into the house. In my head I could hear someone telling me that Richard would be welcome there, as he classed himself as Pagan, but that Karl would not be. It's not that he would be harmed, he just wouldn't be welcome. I sent this to the guys as well along with the three names I heard in my head: Hethra, Isolde and Wiselda.

When they received the names I told them to place their hands on the stone. Richard was the first to do this and said it felt electric, not at all negative. He called this stone Hethra. A few moments later, Karl placed his hand on the stone as they started an EVP session. Karl had a different reaction to the stone. He had felt a negative feeling coming off it. Watching it happen live still didn't prepare any of us for the reality of what the EVP would reveal. Moments later, when they reviewed the recorder, you could hear a very angry voice distinctly say, "Get your hands off the stone!" It was very apparent after listening to the recording that the voice was responding to Karl and him placing his hand on the stone. Once again, stellar evidence was gathered by the guys, but great as that was it isn't the reason that investigation is my favorite.

This is: A little while later they were walking around trying to find a better signal when they started another EVP session. They seemed to get the best signal in the center of the stone circle, so that's where they remained. We were all watching them review another recording session when Karl seemed to get really excited. He kept rewinding the recorder and playing it over and over again. Then Richard went over and listened to it. One word was very clear, yet they were also trying to make out the two words before it. When they did, I about had a heart attack. They had caught an EVP in the center of the Nine Ladies Stone Circle, asking, "Where is Vanessa?"

I could have fallen out of my chair if I hadn't been sitting on a nice comfy couch. It was an absolutely unreal moment for me, but for various reasons many people aren't privy to it. So, here in black and white, I will share it with you. Then you can decide if I should be as affected by it as I have been.

You see, about ten years ago, I went into a meditation trying to find some peace for myself. I was still relatively new to how all this metaphysical stuff worked and was trying something out. I had laid down and was visualizing the chakras and their colors pass before my eyes, counting backwards. This isn't as easy as it sounds, but if you can master it, nothing works better. It wasn't long before I could see, and feel, myself in a whole different place, a whole different time.

I was much younger, with long hair that was partially hidden by a hooded cloak. I was wearing a blouse made of "lawn", a fabric you really don't hear about much nowadays, and an ankle length skirt. I was barefoot and could feel the dew of the grass under my feet as I ran. It was the darkest part of night, but I was laughing as if I hadn't a care in the world. I could hear people behind me, men and women, but I felt no fear. I'm not really sure why. Maybe it's because I did hear both sexes and I instinctively don't fear women. Who knows?

I continued to run, feeling free as a bird. I can't pinpoint the exact moment when the fear set in; I only know that it did. At some point I realized that the people that were running behind me were not running with me, they were chasing after me. This caused me to become frantic, which made me careless. I didn't pay attention to my surroundings and failed to notice the tree that was looming in the distance in front of me. I kept looking back, trying to gauge the distance between me and the angry mob that was closing the gap between us, so I didn't see the trees low hanging branch with the huge knothole on it until it was too late. By the time I did, I was steps away, too close to alter my path, even though the moon had finally come out from behind the clouds to spotlight it like midday. I felt the pain explode in my head as I crashed into the branch.

I came to standing a ways away from the crowd and watched as they strung me up and hung me from the very tree I had run into. I woke up then, the pain in my head quite real. I'm still not sure as to why I was allowed to see my own death from so long ago, but I'm glad I did. I knew it was important then, but I did not know why. Now I do.

You see, the Nine Ladies Stone Circle has been around since the Bronze Age. The story behind it is that nine witches were turned to stone for dancing on a Sunday. It's surrounded by forest. I wonder if this is where I was in my vision. I can think of no other explanation for them asking for me. I hope to find out soon when I make my way to England next year. I will definitely be visiting the ladies while I am there.

Another interesting fact, after the guys did their investigation I had a dream about the place. It occurred to me, because of that dream, why the guys were able to get better reception in the center of the stone circle. Before I contacted them to tell them about my dream, I checked the internet to see if anyone else had come to the same conclusion that I had. I found nothing, so I messaged them with a sketch of what I had seen.

The stones are set in a circular pattern with the "head" stone slightly more prominent than the rest. It also has just a touch more distance between it and the stones to its right and left than the others. When you look at it sketched out you can't *not* see it. It's a pentagram. If you connect the stones, like connect-the-dots, as well as enclosing the circle, you have a perfect pentagram. Anyone who has ever done "circle work" knows that the power is in the circle. That is why they were able to get a better signal inside of the circle than out. Interesting, huh?

CHAPTER 13

Ahhhh... chapter thirteen, my lucky number. My son was born on Friday the thirteenth, just one of those little quirky things about me that people either love or find creepy. I have quite a few of those little eccentricities. Luckily, I've surrounded myself with people who find them endearing, now. I feel a lot less alone in the world. My son, who has always supported me, has gotten a kick out of my involvement with the group as well. He will watch the episodes with me and give his input when he feels the need to. This makes me happy, that he feels comfortable enough to do so. I would never have felt at ease enough to do that at his age which, I hope, means I'm doing something right.

I don't mean to say that anyone was doing anything wrong when I was growing up, not at all. It's just that times were different. When I finally came fully out of the "broom closet", so to speak, I was amazed at how many stories my relatives had to tell me about their experiences with the paranormal. It was as if finally coming clean and opening up about it allowed my family members to feel comfortable enough to do the same, at least with me.

I found out that *a lot* of my family has "special gifts". Some more prominent than others, but an extensive list of sensitives, nonetheless. My maternal grandfather, whom I never got to meet, saw spirits. He could actually see them and talk to them. My mother told me of one instance where there had been a priest who had died in the town in which my grandfather lived. He would see the priest often and wonder why his soul was so restless. Why he would not move on? One day my grandfather decided to ask him and the priest said he needed prayers. He asked my grandfather if he and the congregation would pray for him. Of course, my grandfather said he would, and as soon as they started praying for him, he went away. This is only one of the many stories that concern my grandfather.

Another funny fact about my mother's family is that she is the seventh daughter and the thirteenth child so my grandfather used to call her his "little witch". My mother's intuition has always been pretty spot on but, like me, she kept it shut down for a long time because it just isn't convenient when it isn't supported. I have found that it makes people super uncomfortable for you to know things that you have no business knowing. My mother learned this long before I did and began to block things out early on.

After talking to other relatives about this, even more so after they found out I was writing my first book, I learned that others had also been visited by relatives who had passed. One of my aunts on my father's side told me of the time when her mother, my grandmother, had visited her after she had died. She told me of how it made her feel to know that her mother had cared enough to let her know she was okay. I thought this was a beautiful way of looking at it. What a way to find a happy moment in a sad situation!

Another cousin told me of her intuition and how it helps her read people. It helps her understand why people do the things they do.

Another one of my aunts told me of the time when she realized she had lived in a past life. She knew she had died as a child aboard a big ship and had nightmares of it. When the movie Titanic came out it triggered something and she knew that was the ship on which she had been.

I was utterly fascinated by the stories everyone started telling me. In a way, I guess you could say that me opening up and writing *Soulscapes* was not only therapeutic for me, but for my family as well. It seemed to give them the green light to talk about something that the whole world is now fascinated about as long as it stays on T.V. Once it's in their homes or inner circle, they still tend to freak out.

That's another funny thing are the viewpoints concerning the paranormal by both the mundane and the magical sides of society. With the mundane you have the skeptics who believe that there is no such thing as a paranormal experience. They scoff at the very idea that a spirit might hang around because it has unfinished business, doesn't know it's really dead or simply just wants to. For whatever reason it scares them to open their minds and allow even the most remote possibility of something otherworldly.

I can't imagine living that way.

Then you have the magical side of society who see's paranormal activity around every corner. Every surge in a light bulb is paranormal activity. Every rumble and groan in the pipes of an old house is paranormal activity. Every shadow and sound that they didn't make themselves is paranormal activity.

I can't imagine living that way, either.

Now, this is where I become the oddball of the paranormal community. I label myself the one thing that is the hardest to accept. I'm a skeptic. Yes, it's true. Even with my background and the things I've experienced, I still question everything. I even tell others to question what I tell them because I'm not perfect. Nobody is. Even when I do a reading I tell clients that I will be completely honest with them, but if the reading doesn't sound right to them that they are to make their own decisions. This is the way I have found a happy medium between the two worlds, at least for me. This is the only way I have been able to function and not lose my sanity or integrity. These two things, to me, are irreplaceable.

I will admit, this hasn't always been easy. I remember one time when I was working at another clinic about an hour away. I had a patient in the chair and was right in the middle of a procedure with the doctor when a woman walked through the wall and stood at the end of the dental chair, staring at me. I honestly had no idea what I should do, so I did the only thing I could do, I ignored her. It didn't take long for her to become impatient with my choice of reaction and she started to make things fly off the shelf above our heads. As the surgical mask and patient bibs floated around us the doctor looked at me and asked from behind his mask, "Friends of yours?"

I could have melted into an embarrassed heap of dental assistant right then and there if he hadn't had a twinkle in his eye when he said it. He instinctively knew how uncomfortable I was and was trying to make it easier on me, bless him.

"Sorta, I guess," I said and tried to keep ignoring her, which was hard – very hard. I was starting to wonder if she would scare the patient to get my attention and, up to that point, I had avoided situations like that.

The doctor very patiently said that I would be finished in just a minute. He said this loud enough for others to hear, but not so loud as to draw unnecessary attention our way. What a gent! After we had finished with the patient and I had dismissed her, I was able to go in the back room and attend to my business without alerting anyone else to the situation.

That wasn't the only time I had been contacted at that particular location. Not long after this encounter I had a man appear to me, not in full form this time, but in my head. These types of experiences were a little easier to deal with, so I wasn't quite as bothered by it. He was an attractive man, dark in color, with the most charming smile. He showed himself to me in photo form wearing a bright, sunny, yellow polo shirt. He was standing in a park with large, green, thickly leafed trees behind him. He looked happy, so I wasn't really concerned at first. About an hour later I got the call that changed that.

A friend I used to work with was calling for her husband. He was a police officer who was working a missing person's case in a neighboring town. They had hit a dead end and were looking for help in any way they could find it. No sooner did she tell me what was going on did I tell her the man had already contacted me. I described him to her and she said that it sounded about right but that I had described him younger than he was at the time of his disappearance. I wasn't really deterred by that and told her I would do my best and get back to her as soon as possible.

I went home that night and began to draw out what I saw. The images that came to me were more random than usual. They had a frantic quality to them that I didn't really understand. I was getting snippets of wonderful memories at the park mixed with fear, anxiety and sadness. The memories felt decades apart, which was very hard to interpret, so I just drew and drew. I sketched out two portraits, one of him the way he showed himself to me, and one of a hard looking lady. There was no kindness in her eyes. I could tell she was younger than he, but she looked much older because of her rough and bitter looking features. The other sketch contained a shadow figure lying on the ground in an ominous fashion amidst leafless trees and a fence with a "Keep Out" sign posted on it. I also had details written down that I needed to share with the police so I called my friend and told her what I had.

I ended up going with her husband to the area where I felt they would find his body. It was winter and everything was covered in snow and ice, so we couldn't go very far. He said he would bring others back at another time and they would search the area for his body or clues to his whereabouts.

It was a while later when my friend called me to tell me that they had found his body and that what I had had told them had led to the discovery. She also gave me some closure on why the images he had given me were so confusing. The man had Alzheimer's. I had never dealt with this before so I didn't recognize it for what it was, but it made perfect sense. That was why I'd had such a hard time discerning a time frame, why the visions seemed so scattered and random. I was getting memories from years before along with what he was feeling right before and after he had died.

Even though I have worked with the police a few times, it isn't something that I really like to do. I am pretty confident in my abilities and am always honest about what I see, but I will admit dealing with the dead, spooky houses and locations and an evil presence or two is a whole lot easier than feeling the pressure of locating someone who may or may not still be alive. I will do it, gladly, but I will always have that fear of "What if I'm wrong?" looming in my head. I would never forgive myself if I caused anyone harm or heartache, even if I was trying to help.

That's the other thing that television fails to explain properly when they produce new paranormal shows or another show featuring a psychic. Quite obviously, this is not an exact science. The way each person receives their information is different and can vary in strength from one message to the next. As I stated earlier, very rarely are dreams to be taken literally, and this is where a lot of information comes from since we are at our most vulnerable and receptive in sleep.

Many times the messages in dreams have to be interpreted because they are so random and hidden in between nonsense and broken thoughts needing completion. Sometimes it takes more than one dream to get the full message. That's why I always tell people to keep a notebook by the bed so they can jot down what they remember when they wake up. I tell them to look beyond the crazy!

That's what you have to do when you investigate the paranormal: look beyond the crazy. You may be encountering the most certifiably crazy person believing they are being haunted or attacked. You may want to discount whatever they say because you think they are nuts. I wouldn't blame you, because I have been in those same shoes. I have felt the exact same way – it's only human – but you have to move past it. You don't have to be sane to have a paranormal experience, but having a paranormal experience can make you feel, and act, crazy. Never judge an investigation by the person asking for it.

Now, if you go and you can prove that there is zero activity going on or you can debunk whatever it is that the person who contacted you considers paranormal, then you don't have to go back. In fact, you've done your job and have done it well, because not every claim is accurate. A lot, and I mean *a lot*, of investigations will end up with you proving a haunting hasn't actually been happening. That is part of the deal and should be considered just as important as finding evidence of a haunting. This is especially true when you are dealing with a private residence. There is no need in scaring people unnecessarily.

On the other hand, you may have someone who "lets" you investigate simply because they are too kind to say no, and you get capture all kinds of evidence – and they won't believe it. Yes, that happens, too. Some people could have a ghost in their kitchen making a nine course dinner right in front of them, and they would find every "logical" reason they could to deny it. I've seen it happen. It boggles my mind, but I just look at this as a different type of crazy. I don't mean crazy in the clinical sense, just crazy in the way that that someone can deny something that happens right in front of them simply because the idea is too frightening. Be prepared for these things if you decide to go out and investigate. Quiz yourself on how you would deal with it so that you are ready should it happen to you. Trust me. It will save you a lot of irritation in the future.

I have often wondered – and I bring this up because we have been on the topic of "crazy" – if people like me used to be labeled, psychologically. I wonder how many paranoid schizophrenics were actually mediums or clairvoyants. I wonder how many were institutionalized for hallucinations when they were actually seeing spirits. I'm sure I'm not the first person to question this, nor am I saying that was the case for all of them. I know mental illness exist; I've seen it up close and personal. But I do wonder. It would be very interesting, if it were possible, to go back through records and try to determine how many people were classed as certifiable when all they really needed to do was have someone listen to them.

I remember one time when for three days straight I had a spirit sing to me the song, "Don't Sit Under The Apple Tree". This went on until I found the person he needed to connect with. I have to tell you, after three days of that singing, and practically no sleep, I was ready to pull my hair out. If it were a hundred years ago and I'd told someone that was going on, I may very well have been locked up. Kind of makes you think, doesn't it?

CHAPTER 14

This is where I think we should talk about the pros and cons of doing what I do and what paranormal investigating teams do. You read in the beginning of the book about how hard it was for me feeling alone and the need to be accepted by others. Well, that does eventually go away, but in its place comes the need to defend yourself and what you do. You can't help it. When you have seen what some of us have, you can't understand how people can be so closed minded.

The NP Paranormal team and I have dealt with this as, I'm sure, many others have. There was one investigation where the fellas went to an abandoned hospital, a creepy old place that looked like a long-forgotten movie set. The evidence they captured was rather spectacular, too.

I could hear a young girl there whose name was Samantha. I only saw her in my head, but I passed along the information to the guys and she seemed to respond well to them. She was tiny and would stay around their legs, partly because she couldn't walk. They would get responses on EVP to the questions that I, and others, would have them ask. A few of us who were watching and interacting with them on Livestream were becoming affected by the location and had to watch as Richard started to feel what we were feeling before anyone from the team looked at what we wrote. It was all very bizarre, but it wasn't the first time, nor would it be the last time, it would happen.

This particular location was so intriguing that the guys went back another time. This time they caught something on camera that still has me scratching my head. It is, by far, the best piece of paranormal evidence I have ever seen caught on film – and it was live. Richard and Karl were introducing the place for new viewers, panning around the room while talking about the location's history and how it felt. When they brought the camera back to focus on them a black smoky mist thing could plainly be seen rising up between them in a swirling motion before it disappeared out of camera range. Keep in mind, they were the only ones in the building, a selfie stick was holding the camera and neither one of them smoke.

There is absolutely no other explanation for the occurrence other than paranormal, yet there were people on Twitter denouncing every bit of it. It didn't matter that the evidence was obvious, live and without edit. It didn't matter that, even if they had wanted to fake something like that, they would have no way of controlling such an odd mass of darkness. Oh well, you know what they say... "Haters gonna hate."

This brings me to another investigation that I hold high on my list of favorites. We were doing another night at Wards End Cemetery in Sheffield, a place in which we'd already had a couple of really good investigations, including the one when I felt the "lobotomy" type injury. I told them after they got to the ceetery that they needed to ask for a man named Arthur. I didn't know why, I just knew that was his name and I believe he had an injury to his leg, possibly even the loss of it from the knee down. They were there for about forty-five minutes and had gotten some pretty good stuff, but had yet to hear from Arthur. They don't know this, but I was starting to get a little discouraged, like I was letting them down. Then the most amazing thing happened.

They were walking to an area they hadn't yet been and Richard was saying that he really felt like they needed to do an EVP session in that area. I was feeling it too, and started to get pretty excited! Keep in mind, as this is going on I'm sitting with my phone in hand, headphones on, watching and typing on a tiny screen. It really is quite comical to watch. That's how I do all the investigations with them, huddled in front of a little Samsung 3 phone.

While they were walking toward the spot Richard felt they needed to be, he was holding the camera and slipped slightly down the slope behind Karl. Since Richard was holding the camera the viewers had a perfect shot of Karl as he shined his flashlight on the tombstone right in front of where Richard slipped. The headstone said Arthur. I can't remember the last name, but that's ok because I didn't pick up on that in the first place. My mouth dropped open at the sight of it. The fellas got pretty freaking excited as well. All in all it was a stellar moment, but it got even better.

They decided to go ahead and do an EVP session right there, and as they started to ask questions, we could see (and they could feel) a presence leaning up against the tree that was right next to the headstone. There wasn't any negative feeling to the presence, just a mild curiosity as to what they were doing. They asked their questions, focusing on the possibility of a bad leg, and then went on to review what they had captured. I think, collectively, we all almost tinkled in our pants when one of the questions was answered quite distinctly. When Richard asked if Arthur had lost his leg in the war or in an industrial accident, you can very clearly hear Arthur's response as he states, "Industrial." It is unmistakably a completely intelligent response to a question.

It always amazes me when the guys get stuff like this because it doesn't happen very often. I still chalk it up to their honest approach to the subject and their dedication to keeping it real. Those who watch the show will know what I mean. All of us, fans and honorary team members alike, know that these guys will be the first to debunk their own evidence. I've seen it happen and know it to be true.

In fact, on one of the investigations they did, they actually ended the show stating that, although there was some minor evidence found, the place did not live up to the claims made by others. They were disappointed by the fact but not discouraged, and neither were we, because the next weekend would bring a new adventure. It's funny how a good night's sleep and reviewing a video tape can change an opinion.

When Dave messaged to tell us what he had found, we couldn't believe it. Of course, there had been evidence gathered but not to the same degree as the claims so we had all kind of put it in the back of our minds. Luckily, Dave hadn't, the tenacious little cuss. He will comb through evidence making sure to not count anything he cannot prove beyond a reasonable doubt. I've seen him do this live, as well. They all have. Granted, a lot of teams do this, but a lot of teams don't as well. It's just another reason I love and believe in these guys.

I actually believe Dave may be my brother from a past life. We are just way too similar! Far into the footage, he spotted something that amazed us all and made us give the idea of going back more consideration. Abby was standing in the line of sight of Dave's camera while Richard was outside and Kester was standing a few feet in front of Abby. Nobody was near her. One can see her very clearly as she put on her backpack over one shoulder and turned her face away from the camera. After a few seconds the bag physically lifted behind her about six inches then dropped. Now, someone may suggest that a person was off camera and pushed it from behind, and I wouldn't blame that person for questioning it, either. It's healthy to question. However, that wasn't the case. The bag can plainly bee seen being lifted from the top, like an invisible hand reached down and grabbed it, smashing the bag together to grip it and lift it before dropping it. It's an absolutely amazing piece of footage, and I'm still shocked every time I watch it.

It reminds me of the time when my son, Grey, Jana and I decided we were going to drive out to Skiatook, Oklahoma to check out an old grave known as "The Witch's Grave" at a cemetery there. Grey was unbelievably excited because I had never allowed him on an investigation before. I had never wanted him to be in any danger, spiritual or otherwise.

We all loaded up in Jana's car and headed that way. It was going to be about an hour and a half drive, but we didn't care, and we didn't even care when it ended up being more than two hours. We were just excited to get there...until we got there. Keep in mind, sometimes when you investigate places like this, it's after hours. Perhaps it's not always the most legal thing to do, but so far I've been ok.

From the moment we arrived each of us could feel the shift in energy. It wasn't from the grave which, I might add, was the strangest grave I had ever seen. It looked like a cement missile half buried in the ground with forlorn words of love and sadness, scraped by hand, into the sides of it. It really was quite heartbreaking because you could feel the love someone had put into it. You could almost taste the salt of their tears on the wind. The grave was the site we had come to see, but not where we would have our experience or get our evidence.

What we heard in all four corners of the cemetery made the hairs on the back of our necks stand up straight. As if they were playing right next to us, we could hear a group of children laughing, about ten or fifteen of them both boys and girls.

Mind you, this was after dark practically in the middle of nowhere. It was unnerving, but not really scary. What happened next was scary, and I have a video on YouTube to prove the fear I felt.

We had been there probably less than thirty minutes when the incident happened. We had just started our third EVP session when we heard with our own ears wild cries rising up out of the distance. They began to crescendo, like animal sounds but too many different kinds to count. They were getting closer and closer. I went into full "mamma" mode and told everyone to get back in the car because we were getting the hell out of there.

At first we thought they might be coyotes and that was scary enough because, if they were, they sounded mad as hell. After we left the area and made our way to the nearest gas station for a drink to have on the way home we listened to the audio again. No, it was *not* coyotes. It sounded like Indian battle cries!

I sent a copy of the audio to a friend of mine in Virginia and she confirmed our suspicions. Descended from Native Americans and having been around the culture her whole life, she recognized the sound off cry right away.

The most frightening thing about this is that while you can almost expect to capture on audio, even if it's just a little something like maybe a whisper or something, what you don't expect is to hear it with your own ears while it's being recorded.

It was a great night! The best part was getting to take my son along with me, although he did say a little later that we may have picked a place that was a little too creepy for his first time. That still makes me laugh! He's the best kid ever.

One of these days I hope to take him on more adventures like that one. My next big adventure is going to Europe, to Sheffield in particular. Jana and I will be there in less than a year from this writing with big plans to investigate some of the hot spots we have done on Livestream with NP Paranormal. The two main ones we'd like to investigate, of course, are the Nine Ladies and The Gaol.

The fellas have promised to lock me in the condemned cell of the Gaol for as long as I can take it. I want to see if I can pick up on as much from it while actually being there as I did from four thousand miles away.

It's my hope that we can find a castle close by in which to spend an evening. I think a castle would be a perfect location to film part of the documentary we're going to create!

Filming a documentary with the team is something I am completely stoked about. I cannot wait! The chemistry we have as a group will be amazing on film and I really want to show people how we all met and became such important parts of each other's lives, how the connection we have has enabled us to experience things we might not have been able to experience otherwise. It really has been amazing.

I have no doubts that this will be one of the most amazing experiences of my life, to finally be able to do what I have always dreamed of, in a country I have always wanted to go to, and to do it with people who have opened up their hearts, souls, families and lives to me. They have given me such a wonderful gift: the freedom to be myself. It isn't that they just tolerate it like those that smile at the appropriate places and nod their heads, pretending to listen. These people actually do listen. They have encouraged me to reach for my dreams and to realize that I have something to offer. I am eternally grateful for that.

CHAPTER 15

Well, I have reached the end here. I think I've said all I need to say. I didn't quite keep things in chronological order, as I kind of knew I wouldn't, but I hope you have been entertained and informed. In the end that's really all that matters. That you learn something and that you had a good time learning it. There will be some who put this book down and never give it a second thought, and that's ok. For those who are inspired to go out and find your own adventures to write about, keep one thing in mind.

When all is said and done the most important thing is that you stay true to yourself. Never let anyone tell you that you can't go out and accomplish whatever you set your mind and heart to. I never thought I would write a book, or, at least, I never thought I would finish writing one. Yet, here I am, finishing up my second book in a year. That amazes me. I surprised myself.

What amazes me even more is that I have written both books about a subject that used to make me shy away from people. I've written about something that has always made me feel like a freak or a side show act, until now. I've learned through this process that I have courage – at least I do now.

For the younger group reading this, don't take after me. Don't let others make you feel like there is something wrong with you simply because you can do things that make people uncomfortable. Note the fact that I didn't say that others don't have it; I just said it makes them uncomfortable. I truly do believe most people have some semblance of a gift, I really do. I just know that most people don't take the time to listen, or they are too afraid of saying anything. I can't really blame them for that, however, because I suffered from the same affliction.

I just want it to be different for others. I want confident, ethical, unity-minded paranormal investigators carrying the torch when the last of us oldies are gone. Don't be afraid of things that go "bump in the night". Always remember that, for the most part, what you will be dealing with is someone's loved one who has passed on: a grandmother watching over grandbabies she never got to meet, a friend who died too young and never got to graduate with his classmates, a father whose child was born while he was away at war never to return.

In many cases, these are the type of spirits you will be communicating with. Please show some respect. For those times when this isn't the case, use your smarts. Find your weak spots and reinforce them. Meditate to center yourself before and after going into a place known as a hot bed of activity. If you find yourself in a situation in which you are dealing with something inherently evil, and you may, hold onto your faith, whatever it may be. Never allow yourself to be pulled into the abyss. I've seen it happen. It can manifest in many different ways, so always be aware. Know yourself.

I know I have let myself be put in many situations that people would consider unsafe, yet here I am telling you to do the exact opposite. I'm not a hypocrite, I promise, just a worry wart. So, if you feel you must allow some of the things to happen that I did, make sure you aren't alone.

In my defense, I always had a buddy with me. The reasons for doing it this way are simple. First of all, you will always have someone watching your back. That alone is a good enough reason. Secondly, you will have a witness to whatever event takes place – another good reason. I wouldn't have been able to write about half of the things in this book if I hadn't had witnesses to the situations. I wouldn't have felt comfortable enough to do it. This way I can say, "Don't believe me, ask (fill in the blank)."

View it as sort of a sanity insurance policy. People, including yourself, have a harder time proving you're crazy if someone else can verify whatever may have happened.

I wasn't going to include any drawings in this book, at first, but I eventually changed my mind. After what I have written, I feel it's important to show a little more of the process.

As depicted in *Soulscapes*, sometimes the images that fill your mind can be quite disturbing. Drawing them out helps relieve some of that and allows you to loosen the valve, so to speak. It's also the best way to verify your accuracy when you're remote viewing. You don't have to be an artist to do this either. Just pick up a pencil and paper and draw what you see in your head. You don't have to be Rembrandt. You just have to care about being truthful, even if that truth pains you to draw it.

One other thing, and this is extremely important: remember the real reasons why you do this. Ask yourself regularly if you never received any money or recognition for your time and effort, would you still do it? If at any point and time that answer becomes no, please get out of the field. I have seen good friendships ruined in a quest for fame. I have seen evidence faked. I have, personally, been used and cast aside so that another could claim my reading. When it comes to the shows on television – and I've watched a lot of them – I can tell you almost the exact moment they sold out.

I'm not saying that every single one of us wouldn't love to make a living from doing this. Of course we would. The problem with that is that it is almost impossible to do and keep your integrity. I actually quit charging for readings a long time ago because I was worried that I would make someone dependent on me, therefore making me depend on their money. If it's free, I have no reason to alter a reading to make them think they need to keep coming back. I'm not saying that people shouldn't charge for these things, far from it. I'm just saying, for me, it no longer felt appropriate. However, I have been convinced that small donations, if the person wishes and can afford it, would be welcome.

That's the thing with this field, hell, with anything. You have to find your own moral compass. If your gut tells you that maybe you shouldn't do it, that it skirts the ethical line, don't do it. Once you have a blemish on your reputation it is damn near impossible to remove. Remember that. If you take nothing else away from this book, take that.

This will be especially important to remember when you come up against other teams, or organizations, who want nothing more than to discredit you and any evidence you get. I will wholeheartedly admit to taking the bait and charging in with guns a-blazing, wanting to take down anyone who tried to bash myself or my friends. If I'm being truthful, I'd probably do it again, too.

If you have the same instinct just remember to try and keep your head about you. No one will look down on you for defending yourself, but they may frown on the way you do it. And never, I mean *never*, go after another team first even if you think what they are peddling is garbage. Let your evidence speak for itself. If you are doing your job right, then that will be enough. I promise.

Now, it's late, and I find that I've grown increasingly tired of talking about myself. I bid you all a lovely day or night, whichever it may be and wherever you are. I wish nothing but the sweetest dreams for you.

And if those dreams should happen to turn into nightmares, don't forget your notebook!

SOULSCAPES

The following pages contain examples of Soulscapes as described in the book and as depicted in my first.

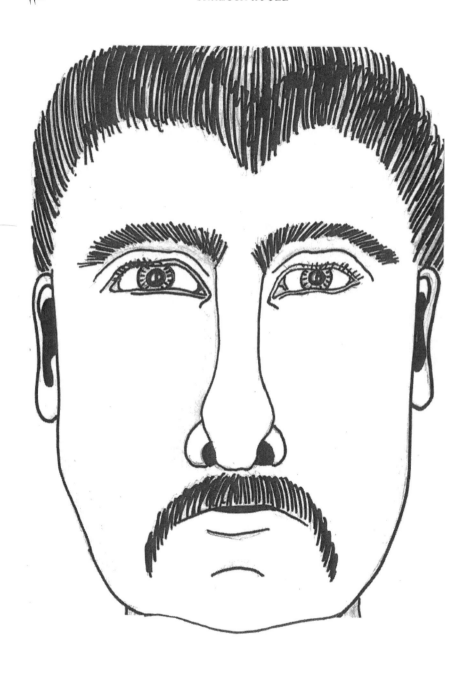

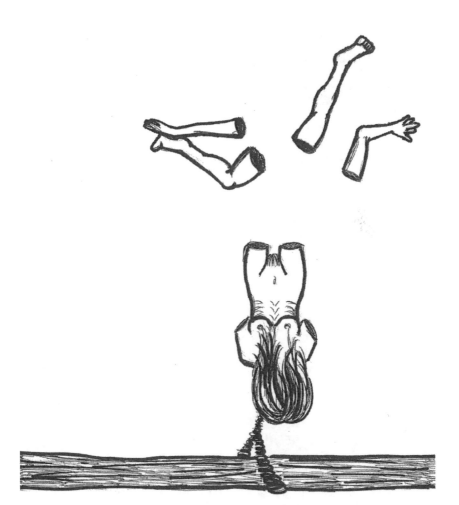

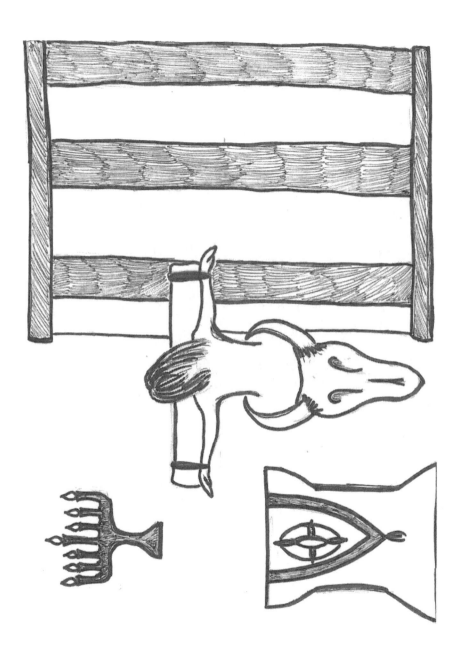

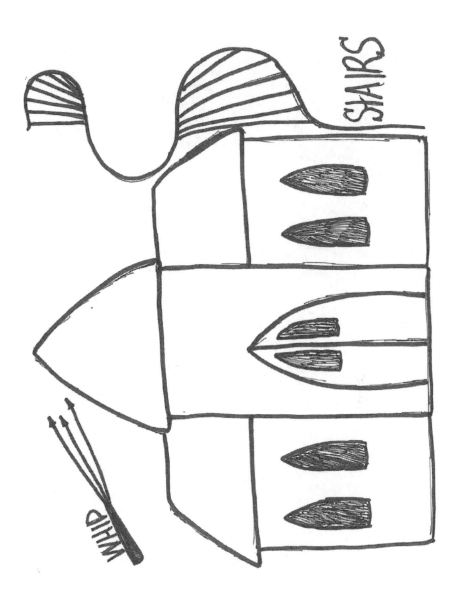

ABOUT THE AUTHOR

Vanessa Hogle has been involved in the paranormal, in one way or another, for as long as she can remember. From talking to spirits as a child to working with various paranormal groups across the globe as an adult, her experience as a clairvoyant, automatic drawer and remote viewer have enabled her to help, not only individuals, but law enforcement as well. Investigations she has participated in have been featured in *The Norman Transcript*, on Animal Planet's television show *The Haunted* and on the SciFixm.com show *Into The Shadows*. She is also currently working with the U.K-based team, NP Paranormal, who conduct a Live Stream show once a week.

You can learn more about Vanessa and what she does at her blog, hottamalered.blogspot.com.

Other Haunted Road Media titles from Vanessa Hogle:

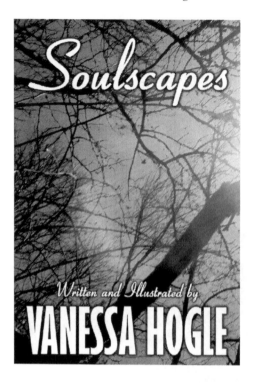

Soulscapes is a journey through the expression of a psychic medium and remote viewer's tapestry of illustrations and experiences. Discover 20 unbelievable psychic impressions through the use of art, best described as soulscapes!

- True psychic impressions depicted via art
- Insights into mediumship and spirituality
- 23 illustrations drawn by the author

FOR MORE INFORMATION VISIT: WWW.HAUNTEDROADMEDIA.COM

Made in the USA
Charleston, SC
07 September 2015